The Parent

Interview with Simone Chierchini

The Aiki Dialogues - N. 9

The Parent - Interview with Simone Chierchini

Marco Rubatto

Copyright © 2022 Aikido Italia Network Publishing

First edition

Publisher: Aikido Italia Network Publishing

Pentahedron Ltd, Tavanaghmore, Foxford, Co. Mayo, Ireland
(00353) 87-13927
https://aikidoitalianetworkpublishing.com

Front Cover Photo © Muhammad Khedr. Back Cover Photo © Tatiana Golovina

Cover and layout design by Simone Chierchini

Proofreading by Lorena Chierchini

Some of the images utilized in this book were found online. Despite our best efforts, we could not locate the correct copyright holder. No challenge to copyright is intended

No part of this book can be reproduced or used in any form or by any means without prior written permission of the publisher

ISBN: 9798401789099

Imprint: Independently published on Amazon KDP

Marco Rubatto

The Parent
Interview with Simone Chierchini

Aikido Italia Network Publishing

Table of Contents

Introduction	7
A Life in Aikidō	11
Practising in this 'Out of Time' Time	21
Good Blood Does Not Lie	27
The Role of the Aikidō Teacher	39
A Reflection on Katageiko in Aikidō	45
"The World Is Beautiful Because It Is Varied"	55
Pandemic Stories	75
Aikido Italia Network Yesterday, Today & Tomorrow	83
Supplements:	
The Great Old Man – Interview with Danilo Chierchini	91
The Lioness - Interview with Carla Simoncini	113

Introduction

Simone Chierchini did not choose Budō, he "was there". On the scene for the past 50 years and in an enviable position in the community as the son of his most famous parents - Danilo Chierchini, founding member and former president of the Italian Aikikai, and Carla Simoncini, the first Italian *aikidōka* to receive the grade of *nidan* - he had the opportunity of witnessing first-hand the major events that accompanied the birth and development of Aikidō in Italy.

As a young child he practised *Jūdō* in his father's *dōjō*, then in 1972 he began to study Aikidō under the guidance of Hiroshi Tada at the Central Dojo of the Italian Aikikai in Rome. When Tada *sensei* returned to Japan, Simone continued to practice with Hideki Hosokawa (1974-1984). In 1985 he moved to Milan where he studied with Yoji Fujimoto (1985-1990). In 1989 he accompanied Fujimoto sensei as an assistant at the World Games in Karlsruhe (Germany).

From 1984 to 1990 he was editor-in-chief of *Aikido* and *Spirito del Giappone*, published by the Italian Aikikai. In 1990 he edited the Italian version of *Aikido* by Kisshomaru Ueshiba for Edizioni Mediterranee.

In 1991 he opened Aikido Dojo Katharsis in Milan, his first personal dōjō, and began practising *Tenshin Shoden*

Katori Shinto Ryu with Claudio Regoli and Luisa Raini.

In 1996 he moved to Ireland, where he founded and directed the Aikido Organisation of Ireland, an organisation officially recognised by the Aikikai Foundation (2001), contributing significantly to the development of Aikidō in the north-west of the country. In 1998 he was appointed *shodan* in Katori Shinto Ryu by Yakuhiro Sugino. In 2006 he received the appointment of IISA (Instructor In Support of AHAN) from Gaku Homma on behalf of the Aikido Humanitarian Active Network. In 2008 he received the rank of *godan* from Hiroshi Tada. In 2009 he returned to Italy and began studying Takemusu Aikidō with Paolo N. Corallini. As a result of his commitment in this sector, Paolo Corallini conferred him the rank of *sandan* in Iwama Ryu Bukiwaza (2012).

In 2010 he published *Narrando Viaggiando - Fenomenologia Comica di un On the Road Italico*, his first novel, and the photobook *Heart's Places*.

In 2011 he launched Aikidō Italia Network, a blog dedicated to Italian Aikidō enthusiasts, which soon became one of the most popular in Italy.

In 2012 Simone became Technical Director of Takemusu Aikidō Egypt and took up regular visits to Egypt. In 2017 he returned to Ireland and founded Aikidō Ireland Dojo, based in Co. Mayo.

In 2021 he started Aikidō Italia Network Publishing, a publishing house specialised in the dissemination of Aikidō and Budō culture.

Simone has been a professional Aikidō teacher for over twenty years and has held numerous seminars in Italy and abroad, visiting Egypt, France, Colombia, Croatia, Iran, Ireland and the United Kingdom.

A Life in Aikidō

"Hello everyone, this is Marco Rubatto and today I have the task and also the honour of leading this interview, as part of a series of conversations about Aikidō that we hope will be beneficial to our discipline. I have the pleasure of having on the other side of the counter, for once, Simone Chierchini sensei, who usually plays the role of interviewer and who in this by now customary role has introduced us to numerous characters and teachers of Aikidō. Today, in his turn, he came to tell us something about himself. It is great, in my opinion, that whoever creates a format then submits to it, because this is the best way to observe things from the other side. It also allows all those who follow Aikido Italia Network and Simone's work of divulgation to better know him, to appreciate his background, dynamics, and way of thinking.

"Maybe we can start by asking you to tell us something about yourself and your experiences in Aikidō, Simone, which I think is already something quite substantial."

"My life and Aikidō are intertwined in an almost inextricable way. When my mother, Carla Simoncini, began Aikidō in 1964, not long afterwards she became pregnant. Since she was already deeply passionate about the practice, she did not leave the dōjō until she was forcibly taken from the mat and brought to the clinic, because the time to give birth was near. Shortly after I was born, as soon as she was able, my mother resumed training and I am told that she took me to the dōjō in my buggy, from which I 'cheered' Tada sensei's lessons with my wails. As soon as I became a little more manageable, she and my father Danilo used to put me in some sort of baby carrier and hang me on a hook rail which was strategically placed right in front of the mat at the Monopoli Dojo in Rome, where they practised daily with Hiroshi Tada sensei. It would therefore seem that I started doing *mitori geiko* at an early age!

"When I was 5 years old, I started practising Jūdō in the children's class held by my father Danilo, who had been an Italian national champion in the lightweight team in 1956. In 1972 my father decided to abandon Jūdō to dedicate himself exclusively to Aikidō and that was how I began practising it. I was 8 years old and my involvement in Aikidō has continued until today, for almost 50 years. It is easy to imagine how my commitment on the mat has followed my personal circumstances, with times of intense participation and moments of lower enthusiasm, following the ups and downs of life. Throughout these long 50 years, however, Aikidō has always been one of the founding elements of my life.

"I would like to mention four specific phases of my Aikidō formation, which I remember with great pleasure. During my training period in Rome as an adolescent, at the Central Dojo of the Italian Aikikai, I began to discover myself through Aikidō and at the same time to get a taste for being on the mat. I studied with Hosokawa sensei and my *senpai*, my father Danilo Chierchini, Roberto Candido and Ivano Zintu. I remember very crowded lessons, a frenzied rhythm and very little philosophy of Aikidō. One trained and did not ask questions, also because no one had doubts about the meaning of training: one practised for the sake of

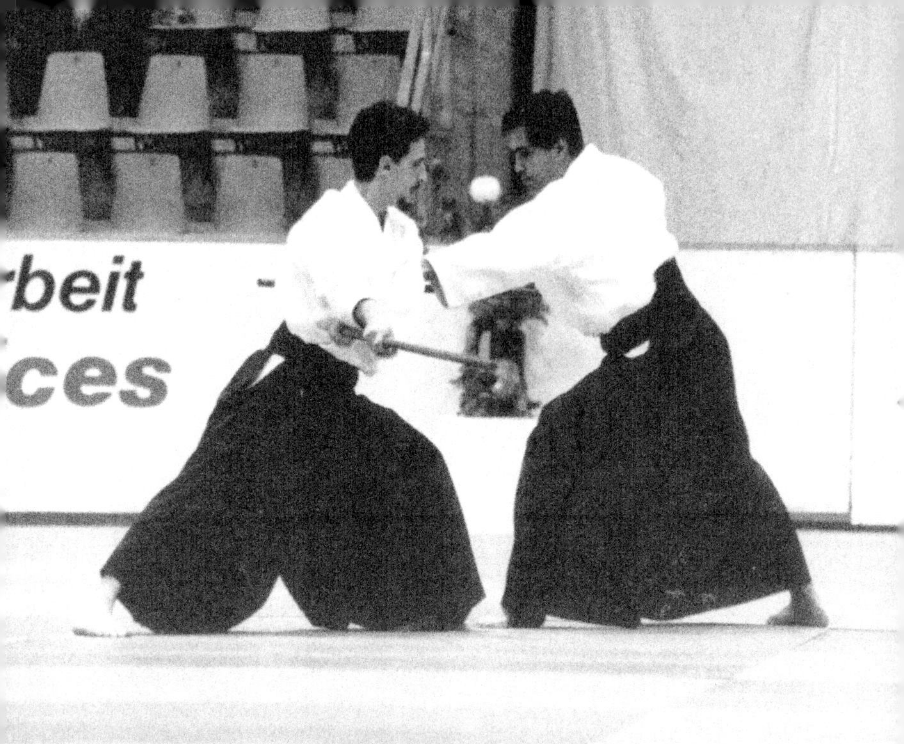
rbeit
ces

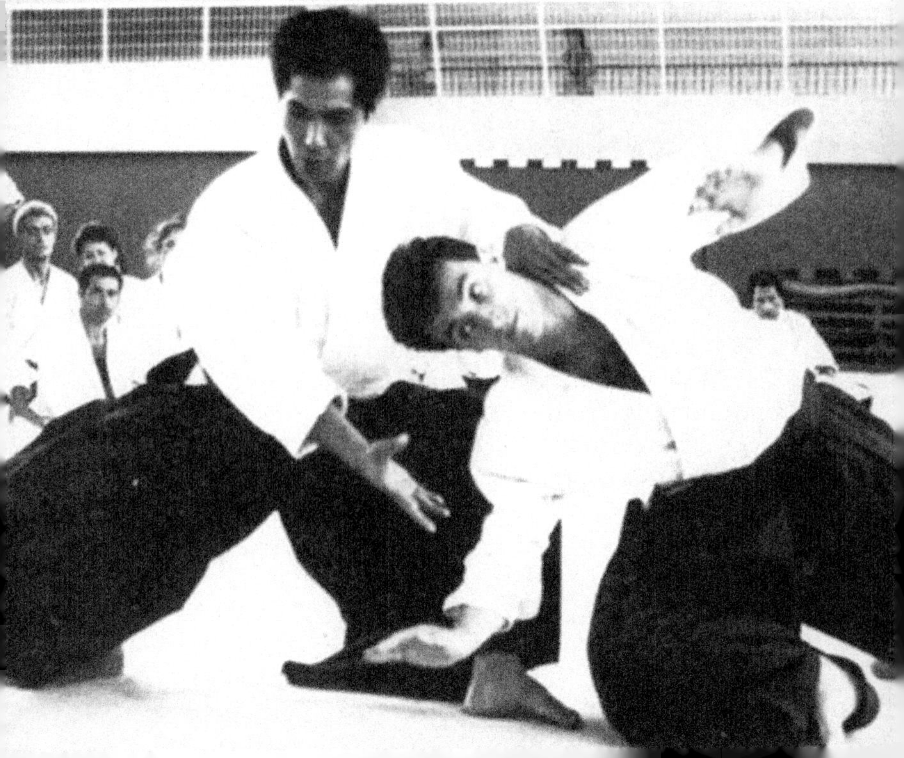

The Parent

it. This period culminated with my promotion to shodan by Tada sensei during the seminar held in 1984 to celebrate his 20th year of teaching in Italy, curiously enough at almost the exact same time as my 20th birthday.

"A few months later I left Rome and my family and moved to Milan to study Aikidō in Yoji Fujimoto sensei's dōjō. This was the beginning of a five-year period, during which I had the great fortune to live in close contact with Fujimoto sensei. I cannot say that I was one of his *uchi-deshi*, since uchi-deshi no longer exist even at the Hombu Dojo, but I was as much one of his uchi-deshi as one can be in Italy at the end of the 20th century. Perhaps his personal *factotum* is a less pompous and more suitable term to explain who I was for him: I did everything from cleaning the mat to teaching the children's class, from managing Aikikai Milano's office (the dōjō at the time had 300 members), to serving as *uke* for Fujimoto sensei during classes, seminars and demonstrations. In 1989 I was his uke during the World Games in Karlsruhe, and the same thing happened again on the occasion of the 20th Anniversary of the Swiss Aikikai in Basel. This formative period next to Fujimoto sensei allowed me to develop most of my Aikidō from a technical point of view. It also had a profound influence on me on a human level, given the strong relationship I developed with Sensei: since I was little more than twenty years old, I obviously considered him as a sort of second father. Many of my training partners were also of great help, from my senpai Fulvio Sassi and Antonino Certa, to fellow students such as Ugo Montevecchi, Alessandro Fantoni and Francesco Dessì.

"A few years later, being fascinated by northern Europe and Celtic culture, and wanting to prove myself in a different environment, I decided to leave Milan. Therefore, in '96, I packed up and moved to Sligo, on the Atlantic, in the north-west of Ireland. I didn't have a precise plan or even a conventional job to lean on, but I wanted to practice anyway, so I started Aikidō classes straight away. To my amazement they turned out to be a great success and consequently, without wanting to, without having planned it to any extent, I found myself becoming a professional Aikidō teacher, which I did with good results for a period of about ten years.

"During these 10 years in Ireland I enjoyed a number of professional accomplishments, including training the first Aikidō teachers in the north-west of the country and receiving direct recognition from the Aikikai Hombu Dojo for the organisation I had founded, the Aikido Organisation of Ireland, in 2001. Direct recognition meant that it was possible for me to conduct Aikikai dan exams without intermediaries, something that became more common over the next twenty years. At the time, it came as a huge surprise to me, because suddenly I found myself becoming a sort of mini-Fujimoto: I had left my teacher and after a few years I was doing something similar - with all due proportion - to what my Sensei had been doing. My decision to take a risk, to change horizons, together with the extremely hard work I undertook with my then wife, Lara Natali, paid dividends.

"Again, let's fast-forward. Several years later, in 2009, I let the nostalgia for Italy, the *Bel Paese*, the sun, the good food and the many beautiful Italian things finally get the upper hand and decided to return to my homeland. Like many emigrants before me, I thought that when I went back I would find that wonderful country that in my memory, or at least in my imagination, I had left 13 years before. The culture shock was dreadful, and once I returned to live permanently in Italy after such a long absence, I found myself really out of place. I no longer identified with the civil society that had emerged post-Berlusconi, which did not correspond in any way to my memories and values.

"This was probably also due to the fact that my Irish experience had changed my approach and perspective on what really matters in life. I tried to reintegrate, but it never really worked out. Despite this, there were many positive

aspects to that period. I was lucky enough to meet and associate with Paolo Corallini sensei and study Takemusu Aikido with him. It was a fruitful learning experience, which allowed me to considerably improve my understanding of the art, especially in terms of *Bukiwaza*. I founded my blog, Aikido Italia Network, and on the related Facebook group, together with you, Marco, and many other Aiki friends, we started a new season of dialogue and exchange for Italian Aikidō. However, I felt the call of Ireland and eventually, in 2017, I decided to return there.

"For over four years now, I have been living with my family in Foxford, County Mayo, a region in the Atlantic West of Ireland. It is a beautiful and undeveloped area, although it has an often rainy climate. However, it is an area rich in natural spaces and beautiful sceneries, and even in these unfortunate times we are all going through, I feel a bit privileged: I live in a large house in the countryside, on a hill with two big lakes at the foot of it; everything around it is green: meadows, woods... In short, even with the pandemic restrictions and the various problems that followed, despite the fact that our work has practically collapsed - we used to operate a family-run Italian restaurant - at least we are lucky enough to live in a human and natural space in which life goes on quite peacefully. I can privately practice weapons outdoors; I have also turned my living room into a 6-*tatami* mini-dōjō and life goes on."

Practising in this 'Out of Time' Time

"To come to the present, as you also just said, we live in a strange time, almost a time out of time. How do you live Aikidō at this particular juncture?"

"There is one basic fact: in this phase of withdrawal from the normal trappings of life, I have had a lot of time to rethink about so many things. Among other things, I realised that just as when I returned to live in Italy, my predilection for a lifestyle that is connected to nature, open spaces, far from the big cities - keep in mind that since I left Milan in the 1990's I have no longer lived in any city - this desire of mine to be out there, in the countryside, certainly did not help me in overcoming the difficulties that always exist in establishing a dōjō.

"On my return to Italy, I settled in the countryside of Montenero di Bisaccia, a small town in the Molise region; my current situation is not far removed from that reality, with due human and climatic differences, because Foxford is really not much more than a few road junctions. Our dōjō is mainly made up of members of my family - a great blessing - and a handful of local supporters. What's been happening for over a year and a half hasn't helped us, of course; I realise it's been a hard blow to everyone, but it's especially noticeable when a dōjō is new or semi-new and the students are just beginning to appreciate the practice and understand it. The break in in-person practice was a highly traumatic event: it's a hard blow to everyone. Online classes or just practising with weapons here at home did not make it any easier when attempting to keep the beginners connected to Aikidō.

"Here in Ireland, we were subjected to the highest level of restrictions from October 2020 to June 2021, which made it illegal to practice indoors. Since September, the situation has improved slightly, although the legal requirements for access to training have prompted me to desist from starting public classes, at least for the time being, as I do not wish to be forced into the position of having to police on behalf of anyone. I hope to see a return to the previous ways of doing things sooner or later, although to be honest, I have my doubts. I hope that my pessimism is unjustified."

"I can relate, Simone, it resonates a lot with many things that have happened and are happening here in Italy. We have been in the same situation since more or less the same period, and there are many groups that have died or are dying, they have disintegrated. There is a serious possibility that many will not resume practising even now that the possibility of starting to train again has somehow been restored.

"It has been interesting to observe how the teachers, a category to which we belong, have experienced this period until now: to see if they are the first ones to consider that when there is no touching there is no Aikidō; or that when there is no touching when doing Aikidō, one simply does Aikidō in another way. I am reminded of the *Aiki Healing Sessions* that you organised last spring, a way of doing Aikidō for how one could do Aikidō at that stage. During the interview we did together with André Cognard sensei, he

said that a *Budōka* always does well what it is possible to do. Somehow, we all had to discover this thing. Perhaps we took it for granted that Aikidō was just rolling on the mat, which is a great thing, objectively speaking. However, it is probably not a mature Aikidō that in which, if you can wring the sweat from your *keikogi* all is well, everything is fine, otherwise nothing works."

Good Blood
Does Not Lie

"I would like to ask you if you can tell us something about your dad and your mum. We know that they were among the founders of the Italian Aikikai, and also part of the very first group of aikidōka who practised with a certain consistency in our country in the mid-1960s, when the Aikidō movement in Italy was still in its infancy. How did they bring you up to be a Budō lover? What values did they pass on to you? Was their example to be seized by stealing it with good eyes?"

"I would like to thank you for this question that allows me to talk about my parents and their relationship with Aikidō and also to clarify once and for all their place in this discipline.
"I have always lived with the idea of having my mother and father so involved in Aikidō as a positive factor. It was certainly thanks to them as well, since they never pushed me or dragged me to class, although, mind you, I am the first of four between brothers and sisters, and they have all been on the mat, yet I was the only one to continue. So it's by no means automatic, my temperament probably had an influence too.
"My parents were not fools, they perfectly

understood our psychology and never took it personally if, for example, we did not want to go to class, or if in some phases we did not feel like sharing their experience or the passion they felt for Aikidō. For example, when I was about ten years old, we practised at the Monopoli Jūdō in Rome and the dōjō was immediately next to a cinema; it was called Cinema Nuovo. At a certain point, I started to get fed up with the dōjō. I was in primary school then, and some strange things kept happening around me: my classmates were talking about things I didn't understand because I didn't share them, basically. Why? Because I was always in the dōjō, even when I wasn't practising, since these two annoying adults were going there. I was always in the dōjō, poor thing.

"When I was a child, I knew nothing about the cartoons that were around back then, I didn't follow any TV shows, let alone football, I knew nothing about the Sunday matches, AS Roma, the national team... In short, I was always cut off. In the end I got fed up with the situation and what did I do? I noticed the cinema next to the dōjō and, pretty much, I'd leave the house and instead of going to the children's class I'd slip into the cinema: we had a house full of free vouchers, as my father was a civil servant. After a while my parents noticed, of course, and told me not to do this in secret, that I could stay at home as long as I wanted or even forever.

"I stayed at home for a few months, without attending training, but after a short time, not even a whole year, I asked them if I could go back. Essentially, I missed the place and its atmosphere, I missed it so much. I can't say that I missed Aikidō, it would be laughable to claim that about a 10 year old boy... Yes, of course, I missed the pleasure of doing it, but I still understood very little about it. The best nickname I was given by my father, at the time, was 'blackbird', after he caught me whistling during the *seiza*...

"I missed the environment, it was too good: my

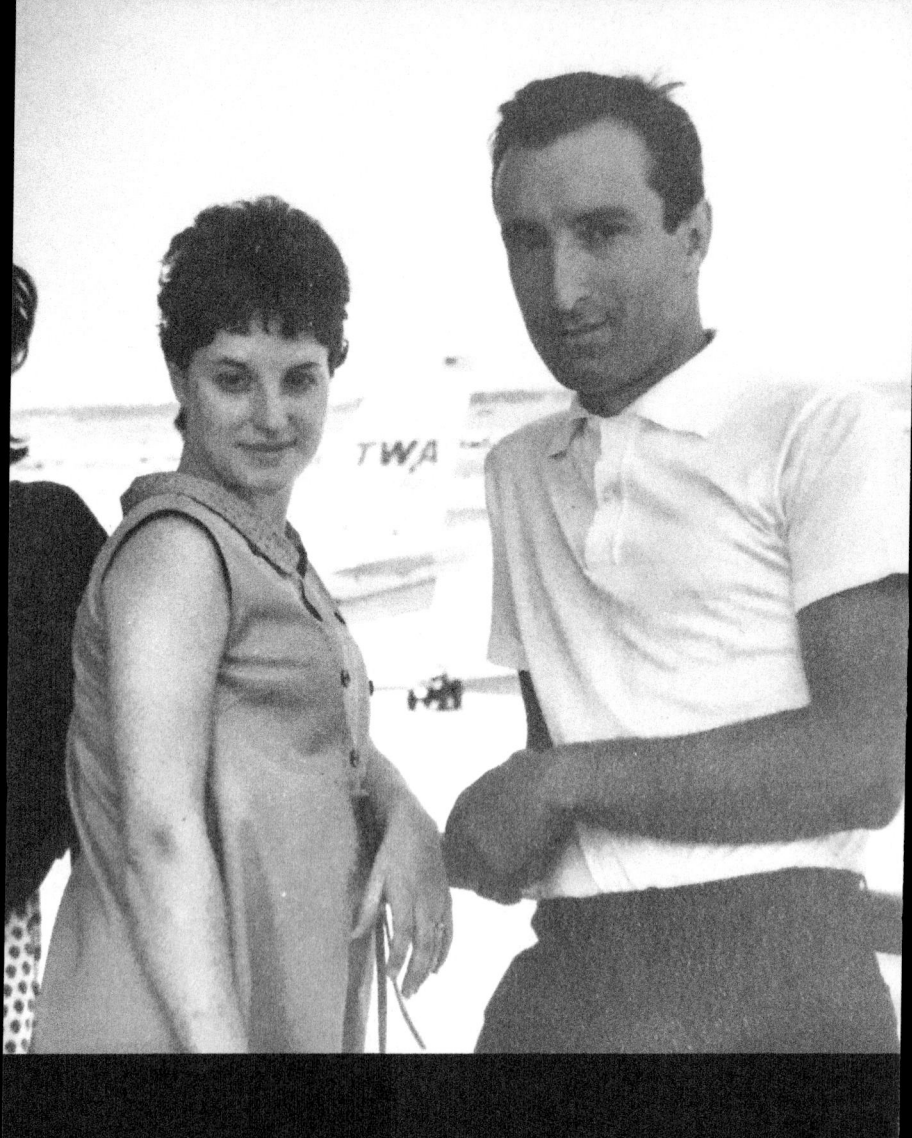

father would take me in the car and we would go to seminars in strange places, and for me it was a wonderful thing, a real discovery of the world around me through this discipline.

"Once I got a little older, there's no doubt that being an artist's son was a huge advantage for me, I freely admit it: all the doors were always open to me, since I was a teenager I never had to ask anyone for permission. Wherever I showed up I was welcomed: 'Ah, this is Danilo's son!'

"To explain with an example, at the age of 18, I conducted my first interview ever, and with whom? With Moriteru Ueshiba - he was *Waka Sensei* at the time, not yet *Dōshu* - who as a freshly licensed driver I took sightseeing around Rome in my powerful Autobianchi A112: a sort of small metal box, in maroon, just to make matters worse... I lived in this world as if it somehow belonged to me. That's what it feels like to be 18.

"When I was growing up, very, very often something happened to me that I regard with a certain nostalgia today: when I would travel somewhere for a seminar, people who met me would get confused and call me Danilo. They did this on and off for years! I must say that when I was younger it bothered me a little, because obviously I was looking for my place in the world and in Aikidō, and as an artist's son I felt I had to assert my individuality and worth regardless of who my father was.

"And who is my father? Danilo Chierchini is a reserved man, who has always hated appearing and speaking in public; he always preferred action instead. Life's paradox is that due to circumstances beyond his control and will, his teacher, Hiroshi Tada sensei, whom he had invited to Italy in 1964, chose him not for technical tasks but for institutional ones, to which he dedicated himself for two decades with the greatest commitment but the least pleasure. Although he had long been the president of what at the time was by far the largest Aikidō association in Italy, my father never mentioned the duties that he carried out with a great spirit of service to the Aikidō community of the time. Then just as now, when he speaks of martial arts, my father's smile lights up at the memory of the old days as a jūdō competitor at the Kodokan Jūdō in Rome, alongside his great friend and teacher Ken Otani. When he talks about Aikidō, he often mentions what was his true passion, that is his role as the beginners' class instructor at the *Dojo Centrale* in Rome. The main class, over the years, was initially directed by Tada sensei until the beginning of the 1970s, then by Hideki Hosokawa sensei, followed by a *yudansha* committee that included instructors like R. Candido, I. Zintu, P. Bottoni and M. Fabiani, and then by Kaoru Kurihara sensei, a student of Tada sensei. In the midst of all these changes of approach, however, continuity was guaranteed by my father, with his silent work in instructing hundreds of beginners and running the administrative affairs of the association and its headquarters.

"I would like to point out something important now: on the one hand, none of my father's students ever forgot Danilo - they met and cheered him walking around town, people that, after years, he found difficult to recognise, since in the beginners' class of a big city there are so many people who practice for six months and then stop - the first teacher who made them fall in love with Aikidō. On the other hand, as it often happens, my father did not get any special gratitude for the enormous amount of work he did in the offices of the Italian Aikikai. I hope that some might learn a lesson from this (it is better to teach than to engage in politics!).

"And then my mother. Carla Simoncini, in the opinion of those who were there, because I hardly remember anything, was among the highest level practitioners who emerged in the first decade of Aikidō in Italy. It is not by chance that she was in the first group of Italian students who received the shodan from Tada sensei and, three or four years later, she was the first woman in Italy to receive the nidan in

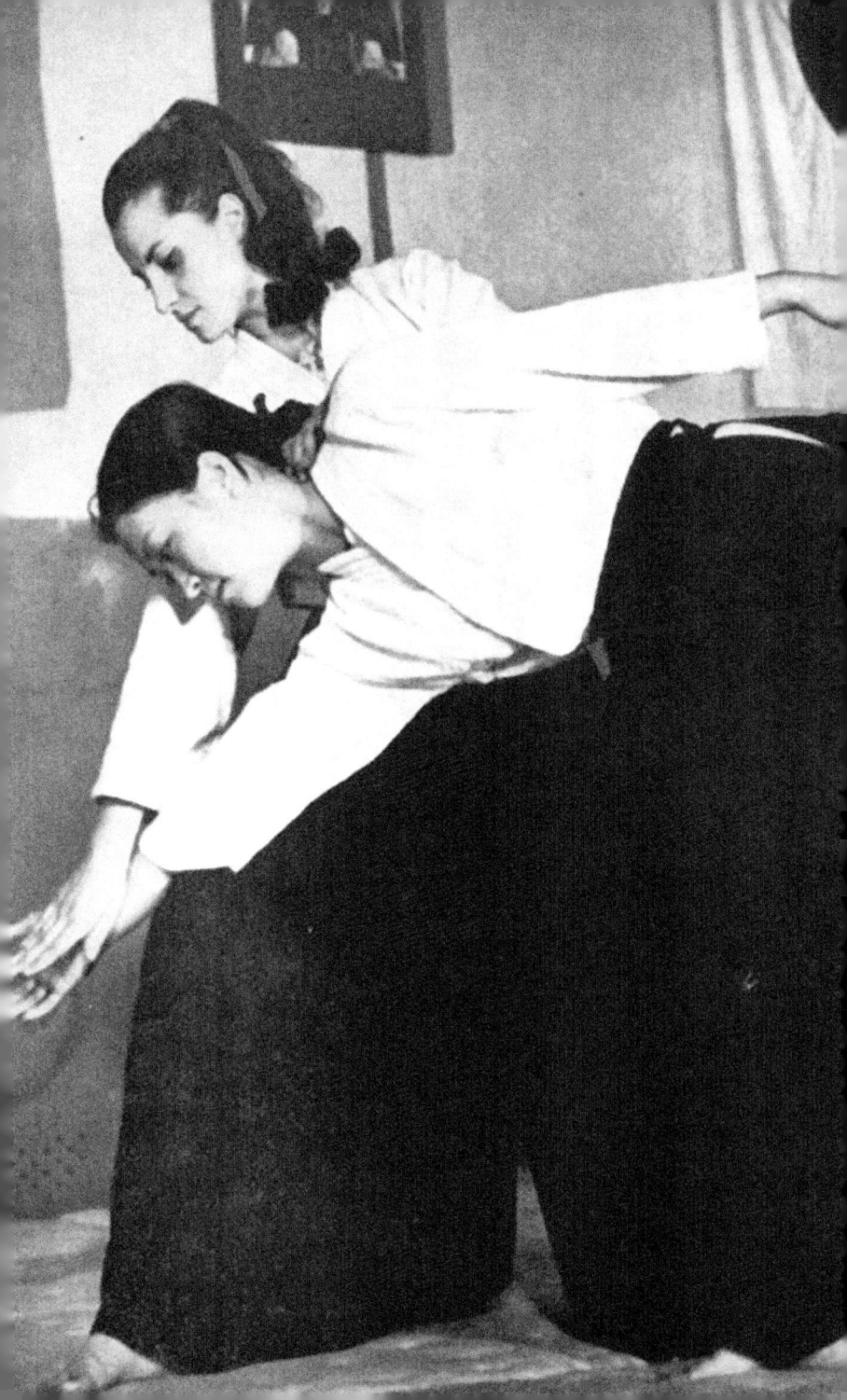

Aikidō. Although she had never previously practised sports, Aikidō was particularly suited to her energetic and non-compromising temperament.

"She was often the only woman in the midst of large groups of men. Do you think that this might have limited her? On the contrary, it motivated rather than hindered her. If anything irritated her, it was when someone treated her differently during training because of her gender, and the punishment for this was usually meted out in the form of deadly *nikyo* or mind-blowing *kotegaeshi*. Several of her former practice partners still remember this. It doesn't take long to realise that, after a short while, where she was around there was no longer any talk of the 'fairer sex'.

"Her very promising career was interrupted by family problems and a very ugly divorce. Once she lost the chance to practice at the Dojo Centrale - it was 1974, another era with other customs - do you know what the only alternative was, Marco? She switched to federal Aikidō, joining what was then called FIK, Federazione Italiana Karate; there were not yet all the other letters [today it is called FIJLKAM, Italian Federation Judo, Lotta, Karate, Arti Marziali], the federation was still in embryo. It did not last long: soon she was caught in a session of piloted fake dan exams that she was supposed to ratify with her signature. So she got up from her chair and left both the Federation and Aikidō.

"I believe that this has remained the greatest regret of her life. In retrospect, I am deeply sorry that this came to be, but that is how it was."

"Very interesting, Simone. Those were also times when it was easy to think that compromise was completely unacceptable, times when it was not easy for a woman to be treated as a woman. For example, I come from a tradition of practice in Iwama-ryu in which a woman who wanted to continue practising was basically required to become a kind of man, because otherwise you could not do it. There were some who accepted this trade-off, while the healthy ones left... It is my thought, because objectively back then it was required (and I am not speaking about the Aikikai, but Iwama-ryu) to rape one's own nature in order to remain in that context. Nevertheless, I realise that at your parents' time this could easily be considered an element of the way, a part of the package.

"In relation to encountering situations that don't shine in terms of transparency or honesty, instead of saying, 'OK, let's see how we can make this thing shine brighter', the mood, which I sometimes still hear today, is 'Ah, not interested'. Without thinking that things that shine often shine because someone picked them up from the ground and cleaned them, and then they began to shine. It's not that things are born already done. Things are born to be done, and in my opinion this is what the pioneers taught us: they went to practice in places with unsanitary conditions that would put anyone to shame and that we would not dream of accepting even if they paid us handsomely. I opened my dōjō in 2016 and I was harassed by a whole series of regulations that would have seemed crazy for the customs of two people like your parents: all they needed was a tatami, a *keikogi* and to get down to business."

"And that's it, in a nutshell. Everything has obviously changed, Marco. In fact, it doesn't even make sense to make comparisons, because they were simply a different society and culture."

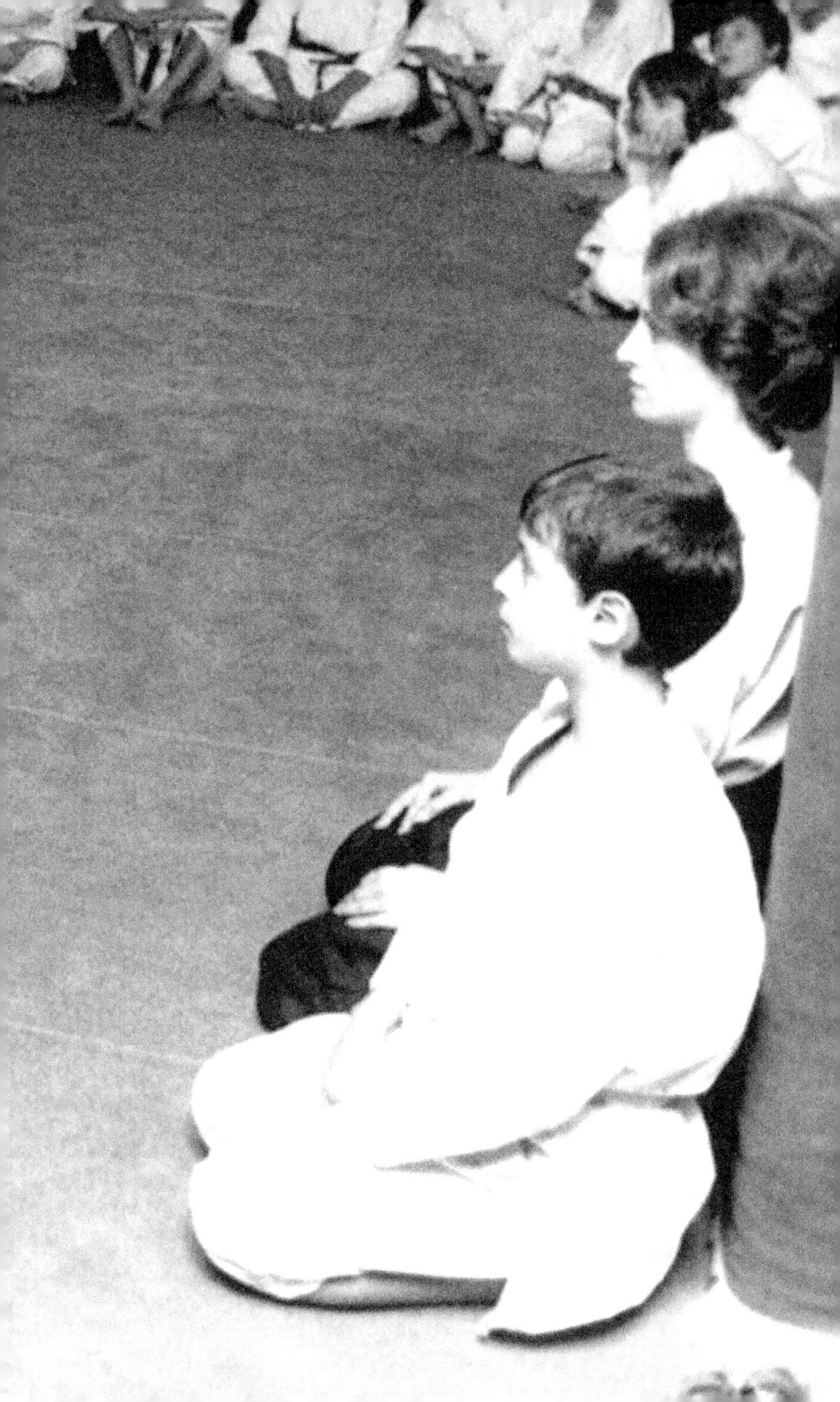

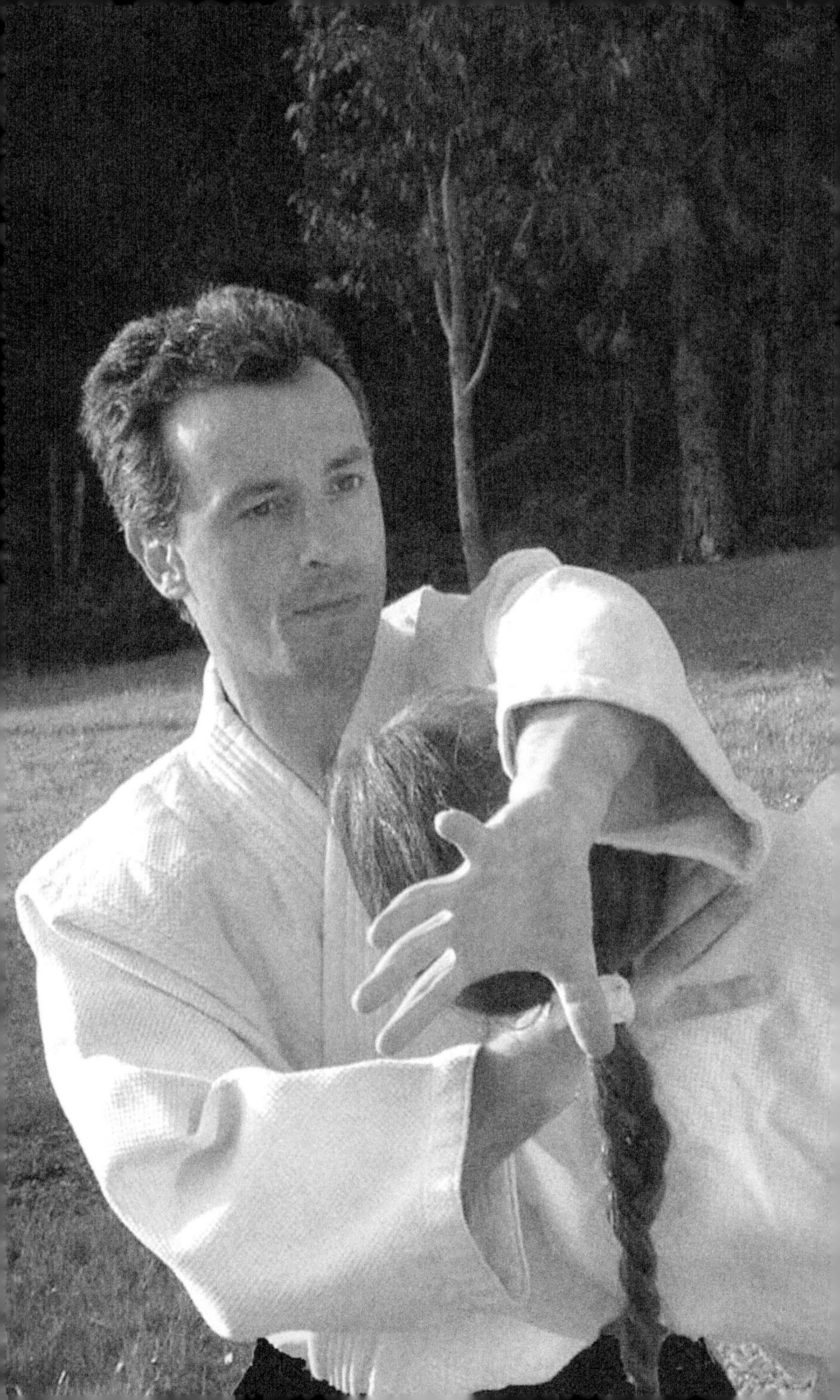

The Role of the Aikidō Teacher

"One thing I was interested in asking you relates to one of the most complex and therefore misunderstood elements in traditional martial disciplines. How do you interpret the role of the Aikidō teacher? What do you think of the relationship between teacher and student?"

"This is a topic I have discussed in a few of my past articles and I have expressed myself in black and white, speaking my mind clearly: I am an 'egoist', I don't teach out of 'vocation'. I don't teach because I wish to make the world a better place, or change people's lives or anything like that. I always trained in Aikidō first and foremost for my enjoyment and personal growth. Consequently, as a teacher, I have never felt I was or had to be anyone's father, not to mention felt somewhat responsible for influencing the lives of my students - for an extremely practical reason, first of all, because for a long part of my teaching career I was far too young to be anyone's father or responsible for anyone, as I was barely responsible for myself. I was still growing and maturing.

"Today, having come of age, I still feel close to a statement made by Kazuo Chiba sensei. I read it many years ago, but I have always remembered it well because I strongly identified with it. I am not quoting it literally but it said, essentially, that in traditional Japanese martial arts, *keiko* is a place where certain situations are created, and then the actors in these situations have reactions; they go there for that purpose! These reactions are about them, not about their teacher.

"This should not be simplistically reduced to a lack of interest for the student on the part of the teacher, to being cold or mean, as it is too easily often misinterpreted. It simply means that in traditional Budō - as I understood it at least, but I am in an excellent company - the teacher doesn't look at all like the old sage character in the movies, who paternalistically is there to shape every aspect of the student's life. I have never seen it in these terms.

"It is my opinion that what the teacher offers is a means that we as teachers manage (being a means). Therefore it is evident that, to a certain extent, the teacher is involved. Naturally, depending on what we propose to the student, certain effects are obtained. There is no such thing as a 'selfish' teacher. Nevertheless, once you have observed a student and proposed a recipe that as a teacher you feel suits him, the effect is something that each person has to deal with on his own. We are not taking part in a children's class: we are all adults and as a consequence the moment we choose this practice and embark on this path, we should accept that we feel something and that those who feel something feel what they feel. As a teacher, you can't necessarily accommodate the Aikidō experience to your students to do them good. It doesn't work like that.

"It is also true that if one practises Aikidō simply as a bi-weekly recreational activity, the entire argument becomes completely different. It's up to the teacher to take notice. The relationship will be of a different kind and the contents offered, besides the practical means to realise them, should be consequently different.

"To conclude, the teacher offers a stimulus and there

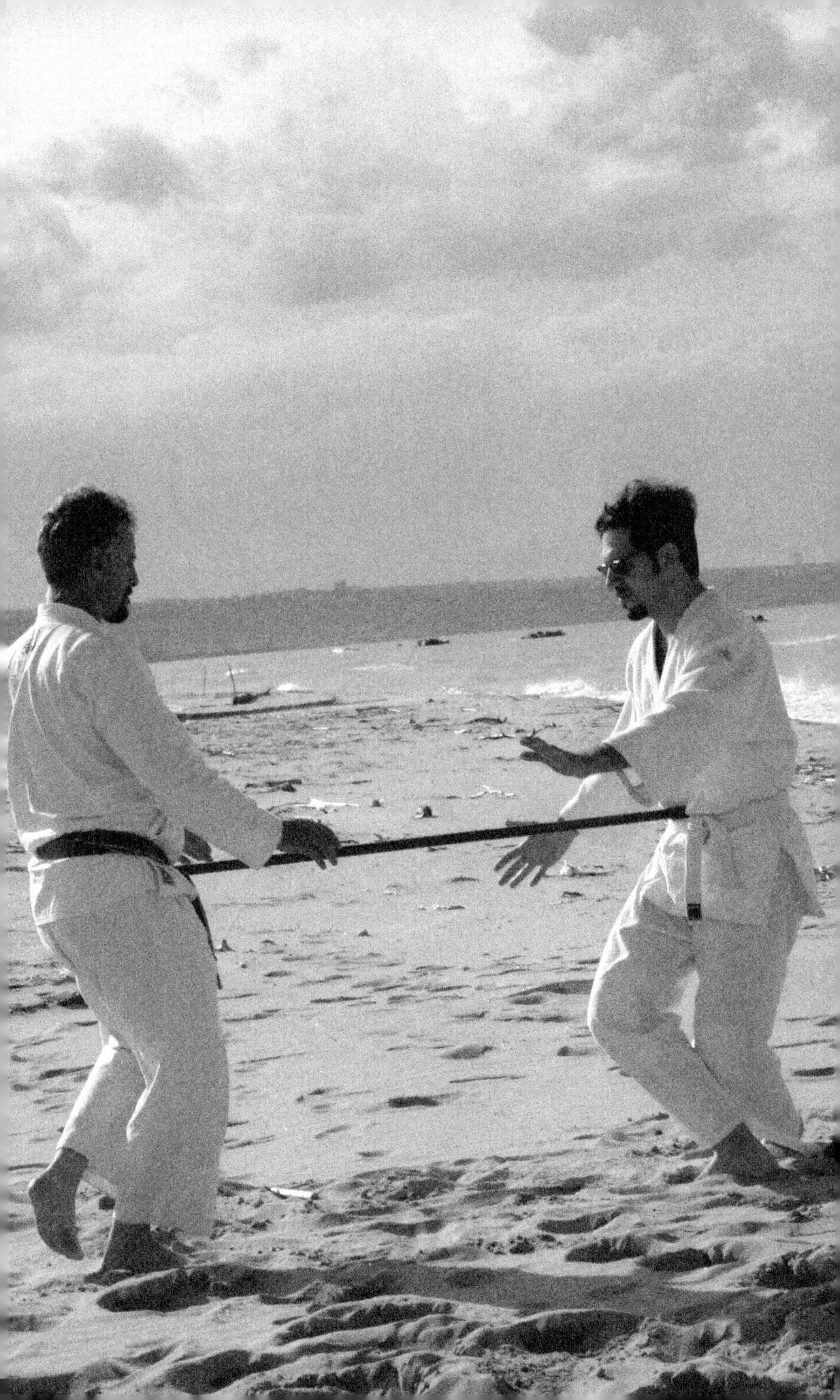

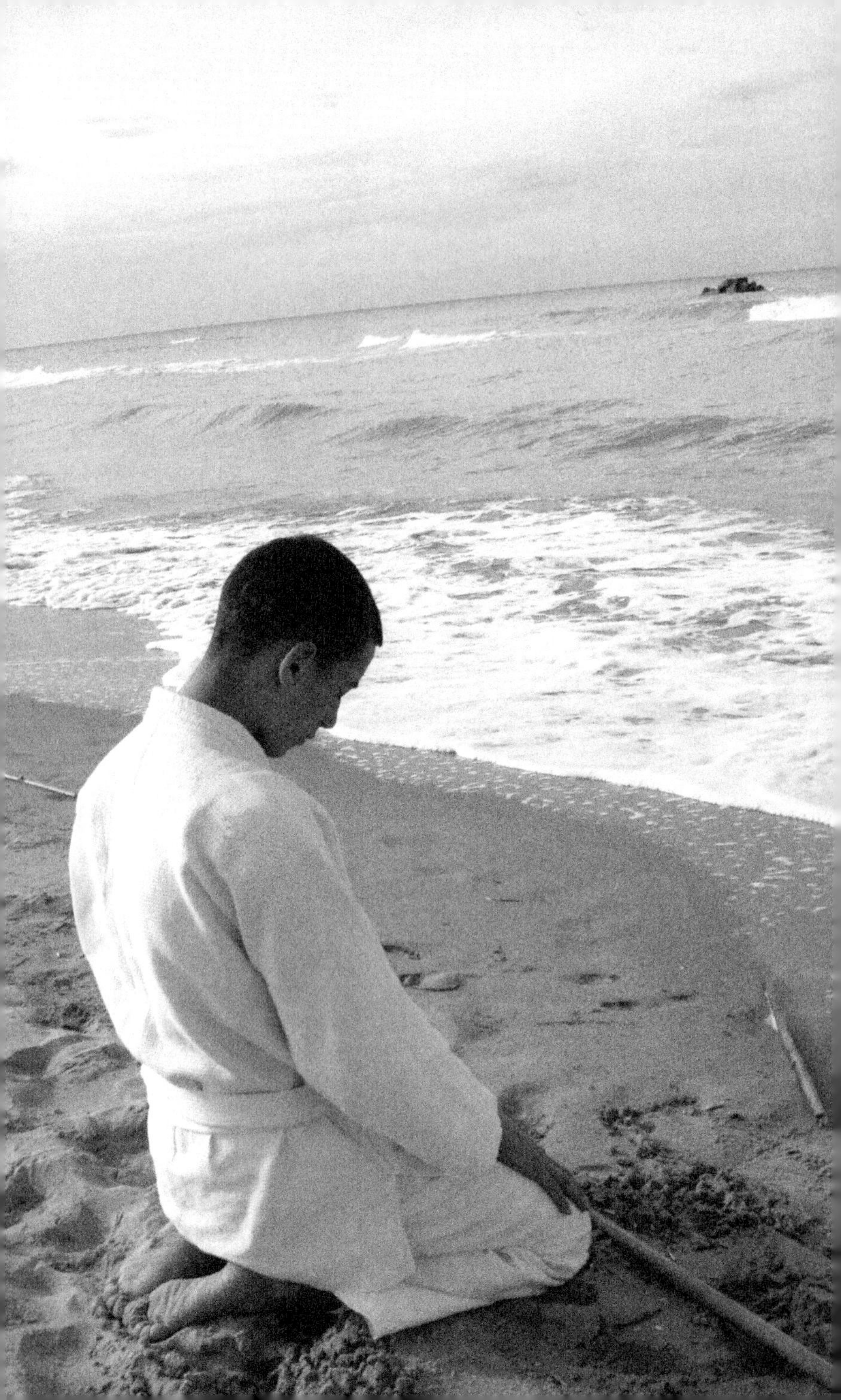

The Parent

he stops: also because who are we? What are we supposed to do, perform brain surgery on the students so that they forcefully conform to what we want for them? I don't think so.

"As a parent, I believe that if you play your role towards your children with commitment and affection - two things that always go hand in hand - and if you live your life as a parent based on certain healthy patterns, rules and values, the little ones who are close to you every day see this and are steeped in it. Twenty years later, as it is happening to me at the moment, one looks at them with wonder and sometimes even with a form of delight, because one realises that perhaps not everything we did was wrong. The example offered was not so bad. That is a wonderful feeling. In the end, with the students, it shouldn't be much different."

"You know Simone, I really like this perspective you hint at, of respecting personal responsibility and making sure to facilitate that each student is the best original of themselves, as opposed to the best bad copy of whoever is imprinting them. It's a bit like the stick when seedlings are growing: the stick should serve to give the seedling a construct when it doesn't have one yet. But then when it has become a redwood, I can hardly think that it is my stick that is holding up the tree…"

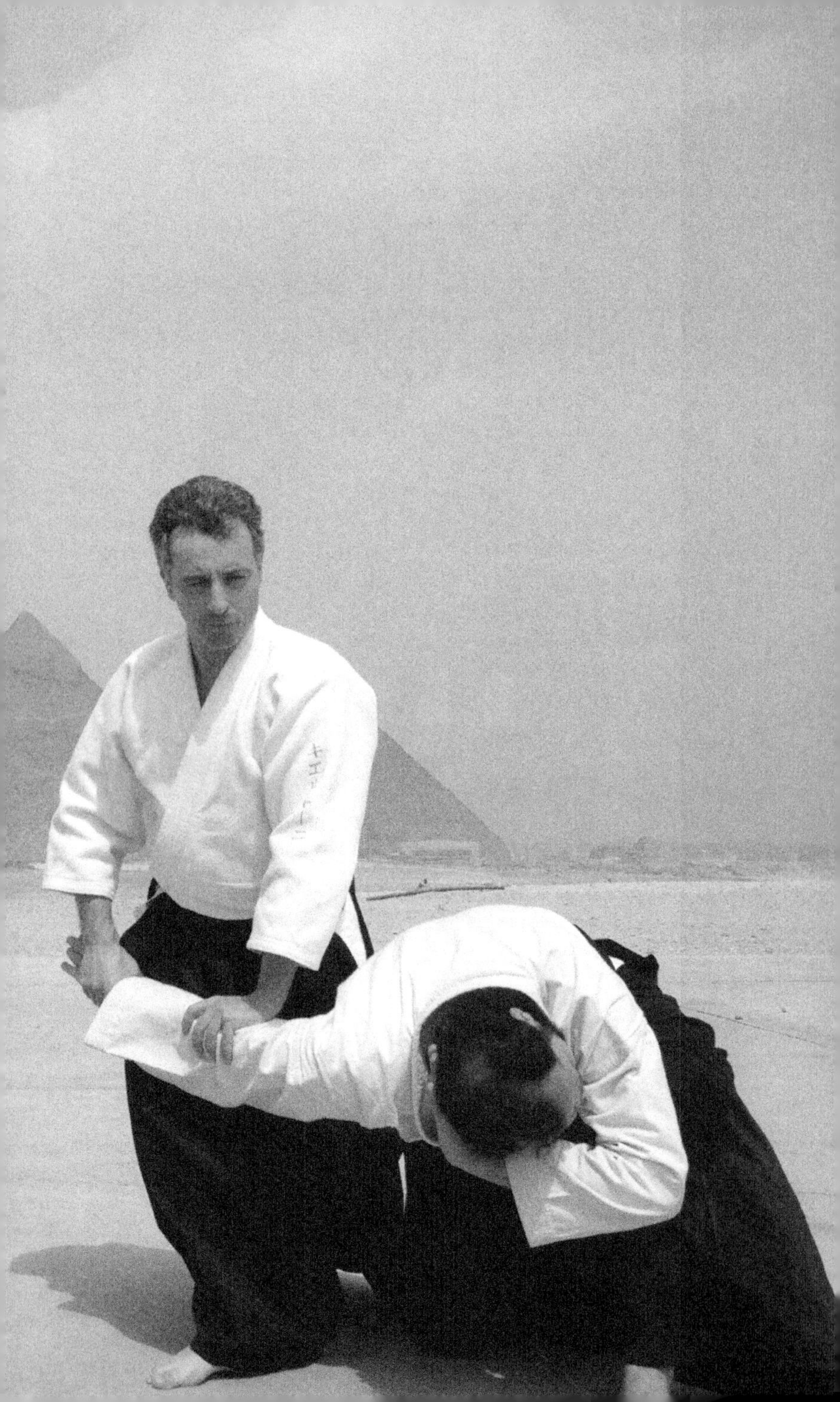

A Reflection on Katageiko in Aikidō

"I would now like to examine with you a matter that from my point of view is at the same time both interesting and thorny, that is, the *katageiko* subject. Aikidō is based, as I still see it, let's say, in 90% of dōjō and inter-style practises, on the repetition of pre-established techniques. This topic interests me because I come from a history in which Aikidō meant exclusively katageiko, while my current situation is one in which katageiko is a very important part, but it is a part, not the whole. I would like to know what you think about the importance of including other forms of training other than katageiko, and what is your point of view regarding freedom of expression in Aikidō."

"Nice little question... In my opinion, Aikidō is a very particular kind of *Gendai Budō*. To begin with, its founder did not characterise its technical forms in a definitive or granitic way, quite the contrary. Among other things, the more we learn about it, the more evident it becomes that in the course of his life Ueshiba sensei privileged different aspects of his art in the different places where he was regularly teaching: in Iwama he did certain things, at the Hombu Dojo some other ones, in Shingu others still. The impression we get today is that he was almost intent on training teachers who could feed on different aspects of his martial culture. If it is true as it is true that Aikidō uses katageiko as its basic training structure, following what happens in the *koryū*, the classical Japanese martial arts, it is also true that Morihei Ueshiba taught his various direct students an Aikidō that presented distinct matrices.

"The katageiko of Aikidō, therefore, is never in any measure comparable to that of the koryū, in which there is no room for discussion or manoeuvring: in a classical school, the correct way to execute the technique is one and only one, in a progressive evolution of difficulties and variations. In a certain way, therefore, the katageiko of Aikidō is a modern one, because it allows those who practice through its various styles to approach different aspects of the practice. It also allows them to begin to develop an expressive form that is already in some way 'free', especially in comparison to the classical tradition of the koryū. In my opinion, those who practice in different Aikidō styles have the potential opportunity to discover the matrices of Aikidō as a whole, and, again potentially, to reach the level of *Takemusu Aiki*, why not, in which the techniques do not occur as a consequence of prior study. They simply happen.

"Having said that, the above is in no way within everyone's grasp, it goes without saying. It could only occur if the practitioner's commitment and related martial experiences were somewhat similar to those of O-sensei's direct disciples. It would be necessary to practice as much as the various Shioda, Mochizuki, Nishio, Saito did in their time, getting exposed with the same continuity and intensity to the best contemporary representatives of all the Aikidō styles. At the same time, one should strive to practice and understand at least at a fair level a number of related martial disciplines - including those developed after the war and in more recent times, from boxing to Brazilian Jiu Jitsu. Don't misunderstand me, this is not to mix different disciplines in an impractical soup, but to build a body and a martial

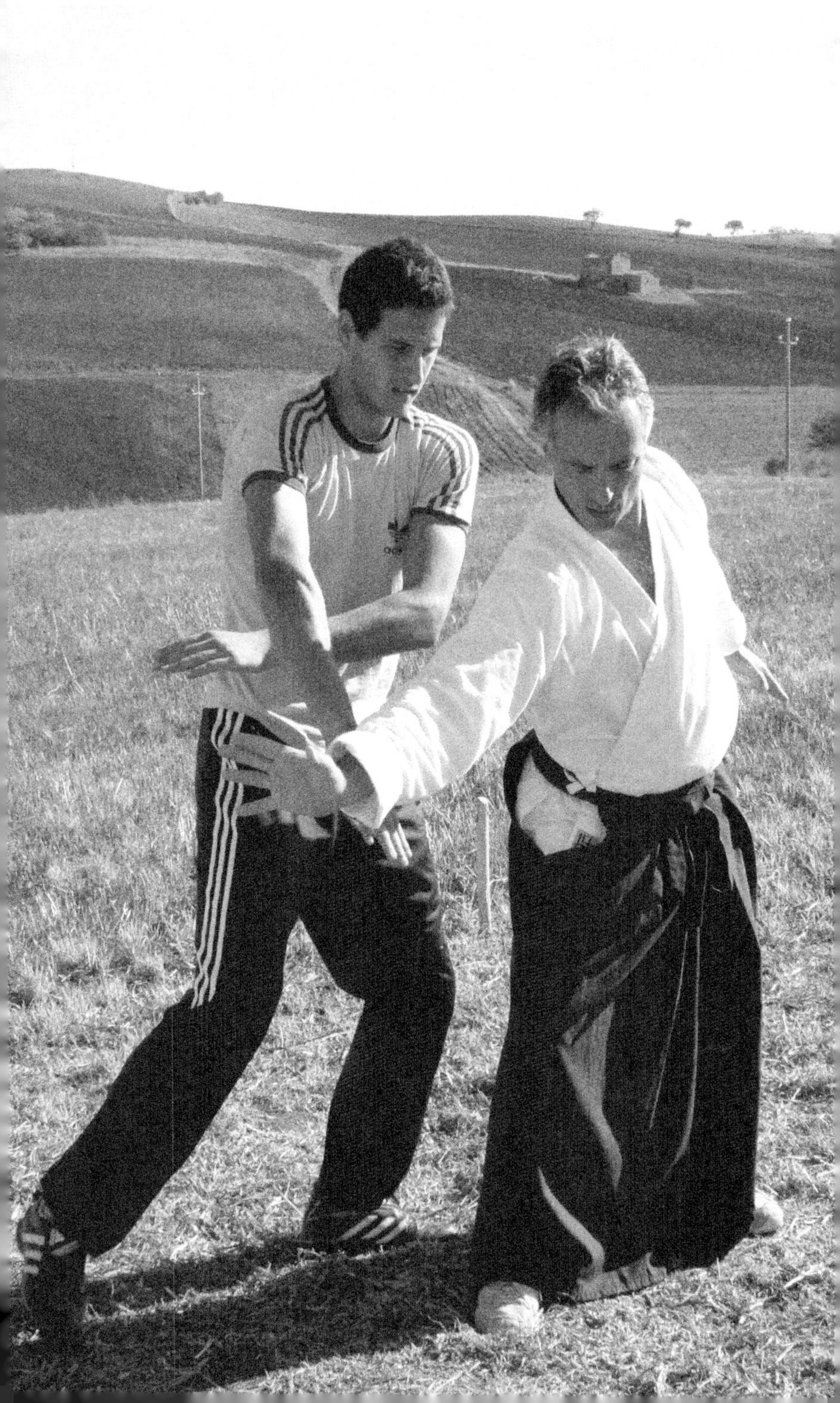

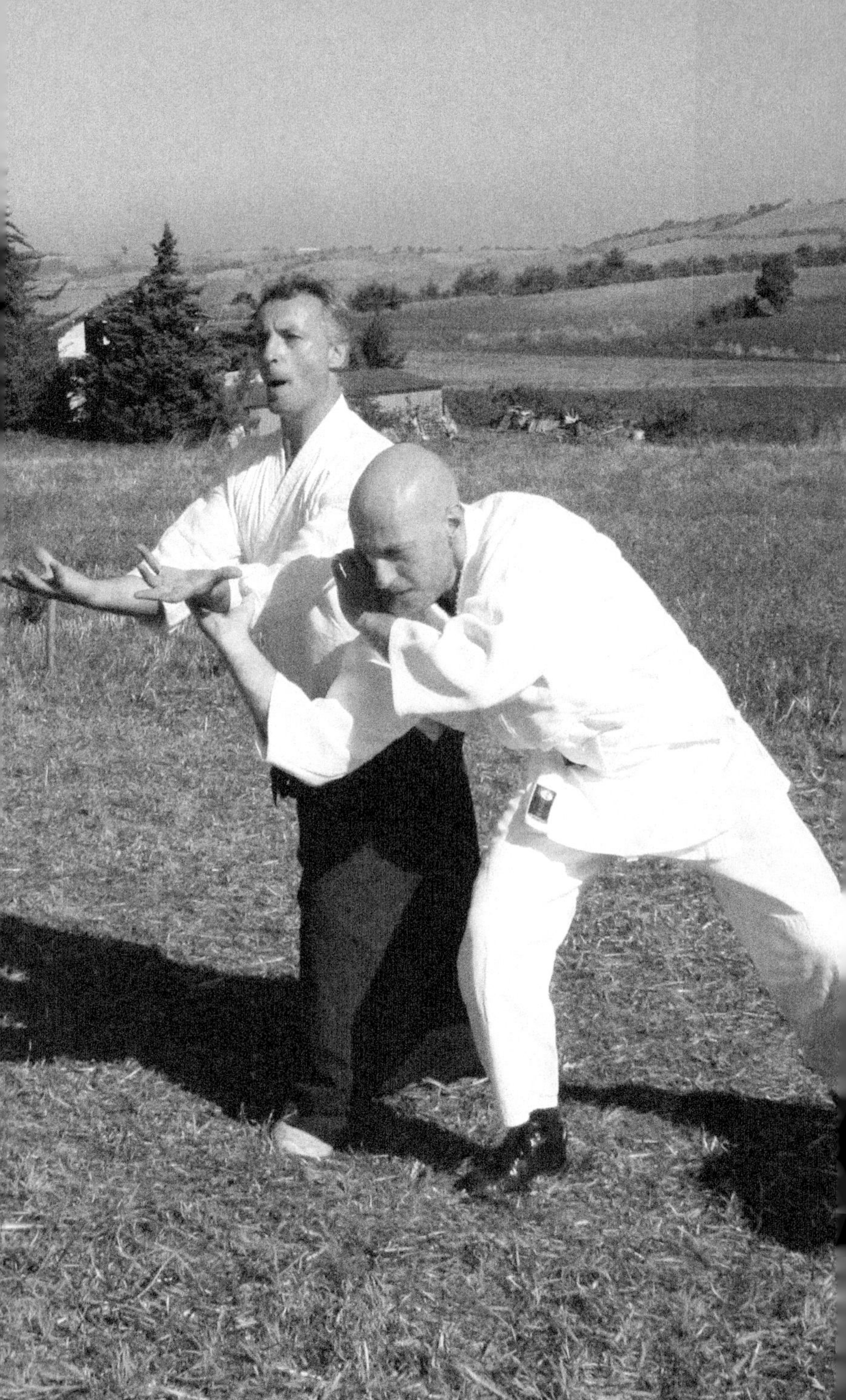

awareness to some extent comparable to that of Morihei Ueshiba's direct *deshi*.

"Whether the above is necessary or of any interest to the ordinary practitioner I have very serious doubts. It could perhaps be a pilot project for a very small elite of young teachers. Alternatively, this approach could be used partially by those who wish to take their practice to truly higher levels, thus avoiding the trap into which so many of us have fallen, that is, to follow exclusively the usual association patterns, whose value, or lack of it, we should say, is directly proportional to the closure of the relative teaching methods.

"For the rest of the Aikidō world, 99.9% of its students and teachers that is, it is enough to continue to do what we have been doing up until now, enjoying the benefits that there are anyway, both on a physical and psychological level, and having fun while being involved with something that we enjoy and that also opens up many possibilities on a social level.

"In this case, however, I believe it important to respect the internal coherence of one's work when presenting it to the outside world. I would advise against emphasising concepts such as martial art, self-defence or similar. If you are practising an art that is basically a relational group activity with a strong social component, which has its validity as such, it should also be presented as such.

"Bottom line, everyone practises as they see fit, depending on their goals. If there is one remarkable thing that has happened in the last decade or two, almost everyone has realised that no one is doing 'true' Aikidō. It doesn't exist, true Aikidō has been over since its founder passed away. What is needed is a healthy exercise of self-awareness regarding our own practice: we should never falsely present its outcomes to the world outside of Aikidō. Honesty and integrity must always be our guidelines. To present oneself as an unbeatable martial expert, when in fact one is studying the relational ability to listen to the other in the company of students who are doing a highly preordained practice is, in my opinion, truly dishonest: just as phoney as talking about peace and harmony while you teach how to stab others with a knife."

"Something interesting that perhaps we could gradually take home, as a generation, is that, as you mentioned earlier, Simone, we are beginning to acquire a collective awareness that whether you wish to sing in the parish choir or sing as a tenor at *La Scala* in Milan, you have to follow two separate paths. The path of the parish choir - I don't mind it! - is made up of people who maybe have some spare time on a Saturday afternoon and wish to use it to sing a little. If you intend to become a professional tenor, however, you have to know music, and you have to seek out various music teachers: you won't be satisfied with studying under just one teacher, but under a whole host of specialists.

"We could probably say the same thing for any martialist or aikidōka: if you are a hobbyist and you go training twice a week for an hour and a half, that's fine, you will have a certain type of path. If, on the other hand, you want to become the new Tissier, who has international responsibilities and assignments and holds national seminars halfway around the world, your path should probably be structured a little more along university lines, where for example the multitude is an added value, not a problem. That's what your words suggested to me, Simone, I don't know if I caught what you were actually saying."

"That's basically it. The first thing to remember is that 99.9% of us practice in such a way that has nothing to do with the founder's way, but also nothing to do with Tissier's way. It has to be acknowledged, one has to accept the position in which we are, and not to present ourselves as great martial artists: we are engaged in an activity which is nevertheless of great benefit, as proven over the years,

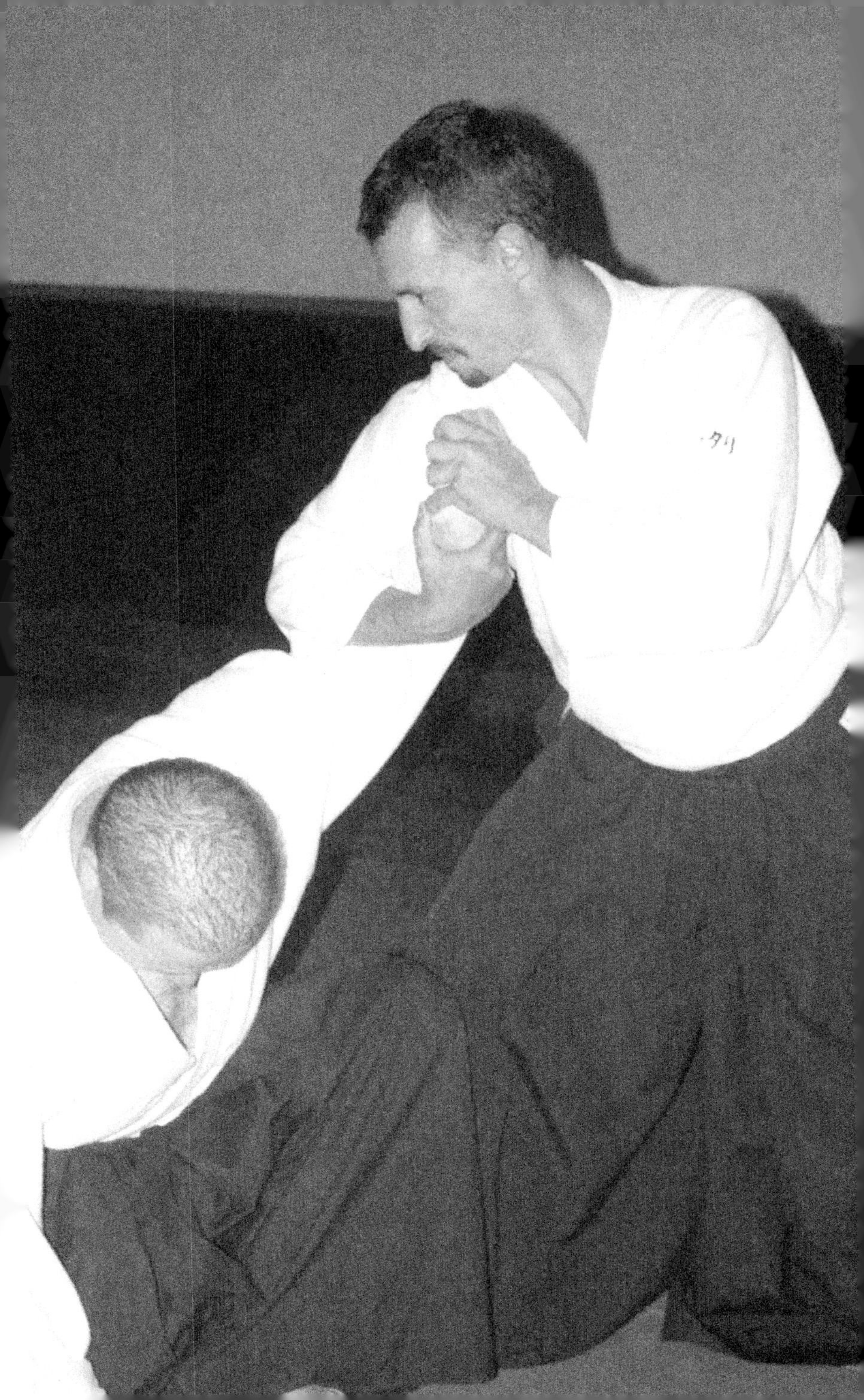

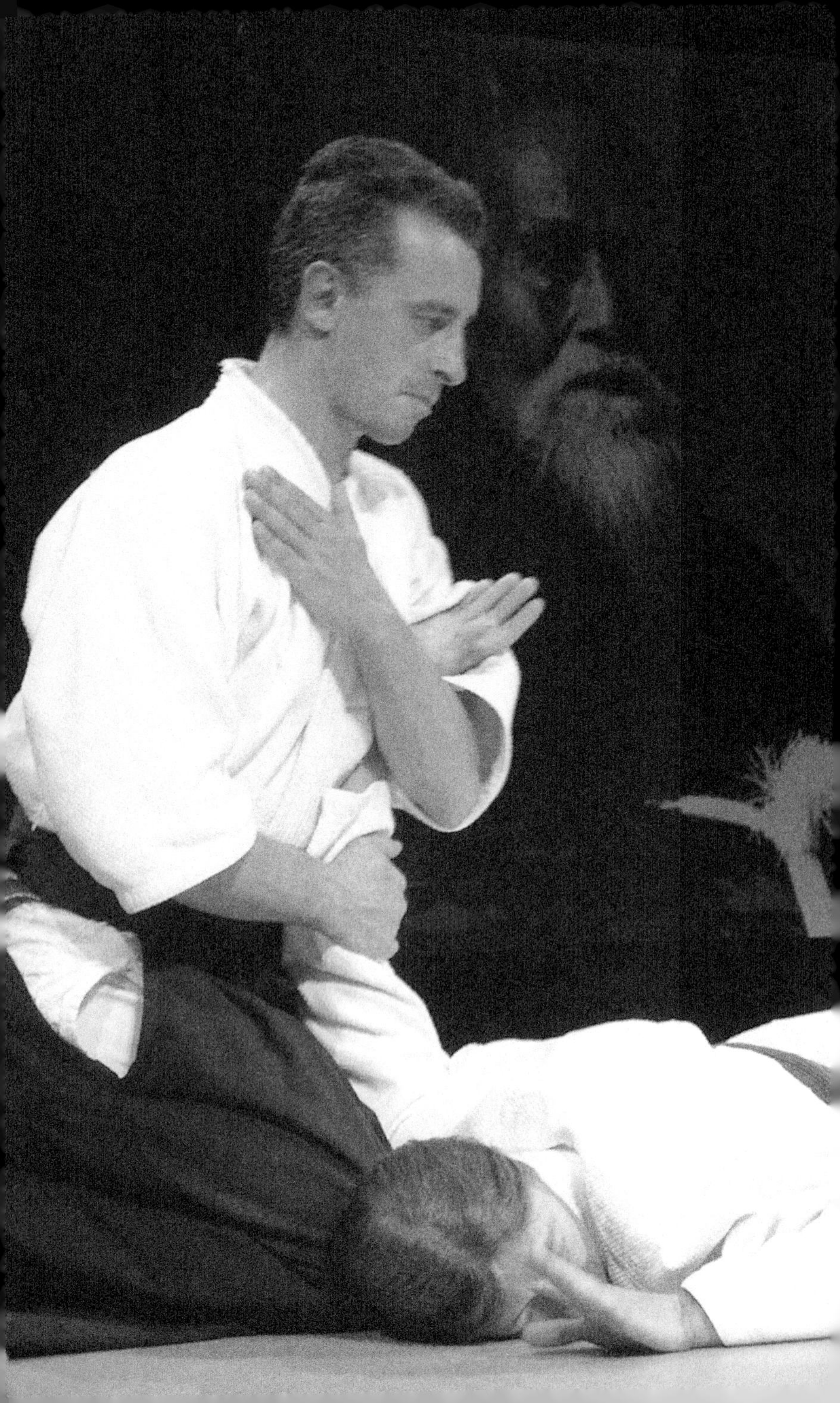

because we all personally feel its positive influence. In short, it is important not to give messages that do not correspond to what one actually does on the mat.

"Next, there has to be, and I hope it will develop further and further, a share of professional and dedicated teachers, who obviously should start young, since it takes time to do things properly. Teachers who aim to reach higher levels, have the tradition to look at: it clearly shows what those who have come before us have done to this end. Thus the argument I made earlier, I'm not going to repeat it.

"We have to recreate the same conditions, and relate them to the present time, because Ueshiba sensei is no longer here, thus, if one wishes to interface with the various matrices of Aikidō, one cannot do so, because from the beginning no one, apart from Ueshiba sensei, has taught Aikidō. Everyone teaches fragments of Aikidō. Therefore if one wants to grow, it is imperative to interface, to see many different things and above all to dedicate one's entire life to it."

"Clear as day."

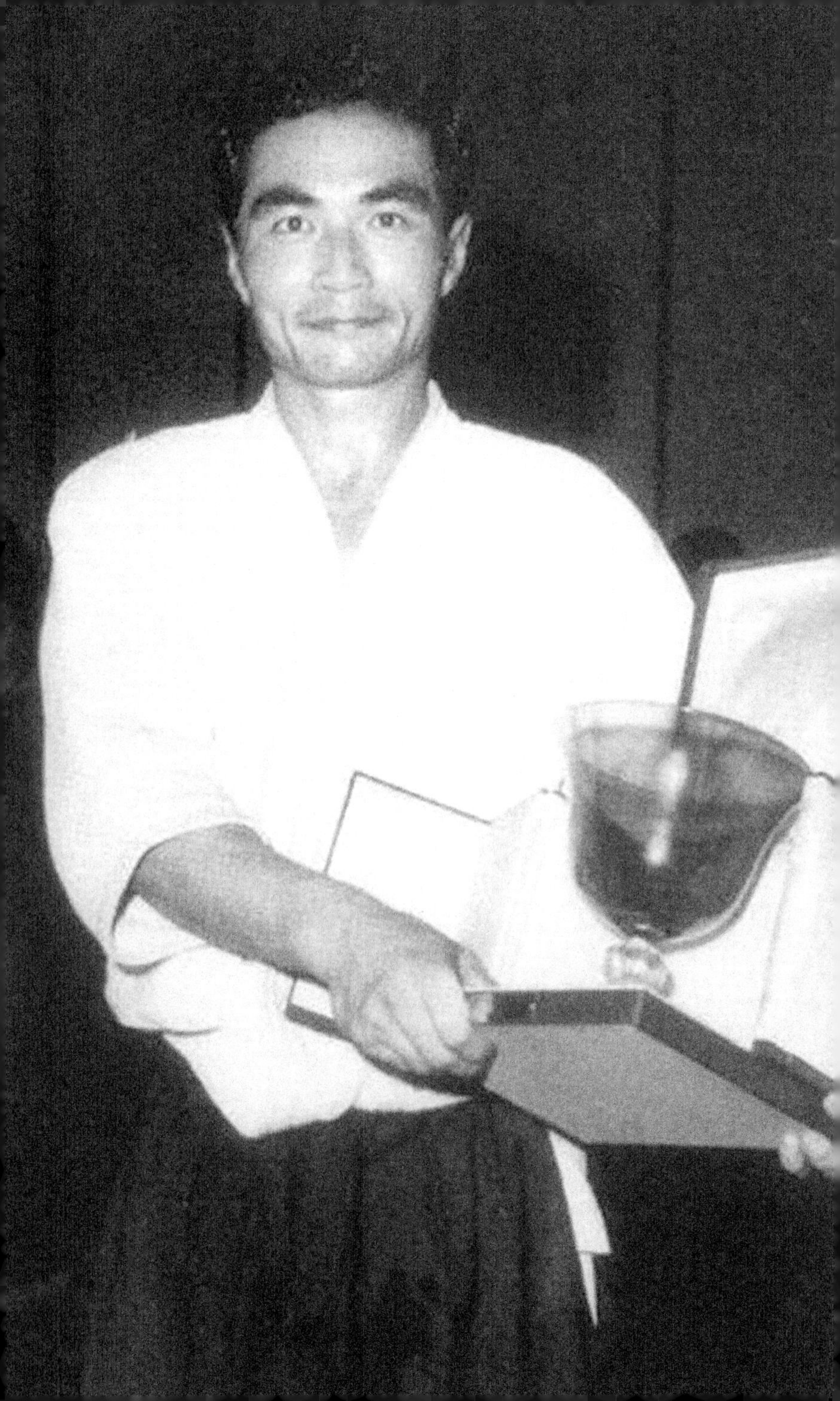

"The World Is Beautiful Because It Is Varied"

"To wrap up the previous topic about expressive freedom in Aikidō, how have you experienced it in your practice and what lessons have you learned from it?"

"I was quite lucky because, as I was saying, the period in which I was developing as an aikidoist up to 3rd dan - a period that falls between the mid '70s and the '90s - corresponded, in my opinion at least, to the golden age of the Italian Aikikai, my association of origin. Even if the official version states that the technical guideline of the Italian Aikikai was dictated by the Head Teacher Hiroshi Tada sensei - this is what everyone seems to think and it is also posted on the Italian Aikikai website - in truth, technically speaking, the Italian Aikikai was not so monolithic at all.

"Besides Tada sensei, who came from Japan to teach two or three times a year, at that time there were two other Aikikai Hombu Dojo Japanese shihan in Italy, and not just any two teachers: Fujimoto and Hosokawa sensei. The simple truth is that it was they who carried out the association's teaching on the ground, on a daily basis. The two of them did so with deep and unfailing respect for the figure of Tada sensei, but virtually without following his technical guidelines to any degree. Tada sensei's seminars resulted in a form of superior inspiration that was, however, inserted into a learning context that was produced and regulated by Fujimoto and Hosokawa sensei.

"From a technical point of view, these two teachers were quite distinctly different from each other, or rather, in some ways they were even opposites, although they were in agreement in their work. That's the beauty of it: they were part of the same organism, they were extremely different, they did very different things, but they got along; in their diversity, they acted in agreement. As a result, for us students, on the ground, there was a diversity in the technical proposal that was not common in Aikidō outside of Japan. Those who studied at that time - if open-minded, because even in those days there was a Fuji party and a Hoso party, which spoke very little to each other and did not go to each other's seminars - however, those who were intellectually open and therefore accepted to expose themselves to this diversity of paths, could do so while remaining within the same association.

"I happened to be in this fortunate position of being there. Let's continue to use my own path as an example: when I started out, in Rome's Dojo Centrale (once I got a little older, of course), officially it was Tada sensei's, who however lived in Tokyo, and therefore the activities were directed by Hosokawa sensei, a direct pupil of his. Yet, Hosokawa sensei did not resemble Tada sensei in any way and did not follow his teaching methods.

"I studied with Hosokawa up to shodan, then I moved to Milan, to Fujimoto, as I mentioned before. I have already explained that the two Sensei were profoundly different. In what way were they different? First of all from a physical point of view: Hosokawa was small, short, loved tight and essential movements, and was a fine scholar of weapons; he was introverted in character, not an easy person to deal with; he had a teaching system based on not offering the student anything to hold on to; every day was different,

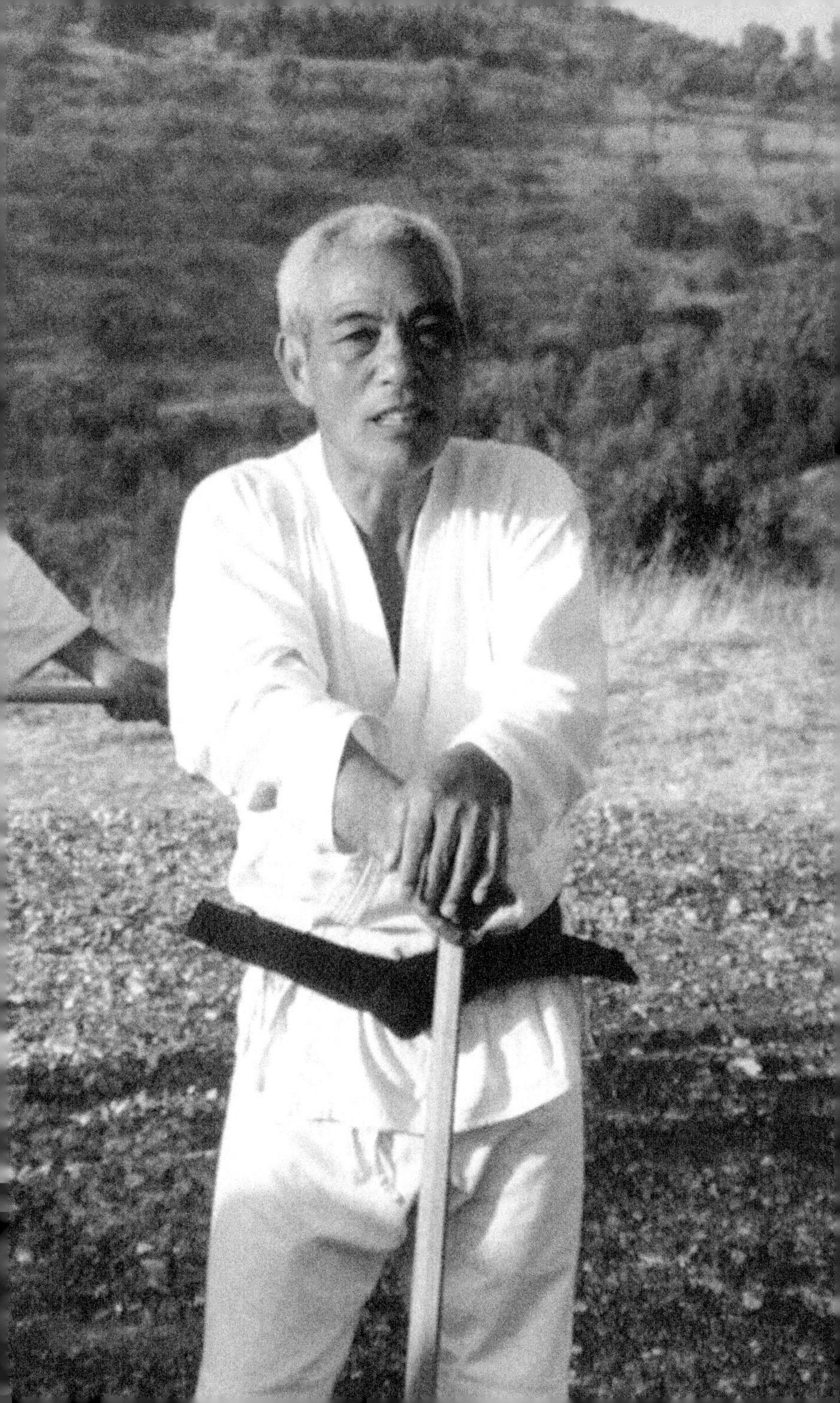

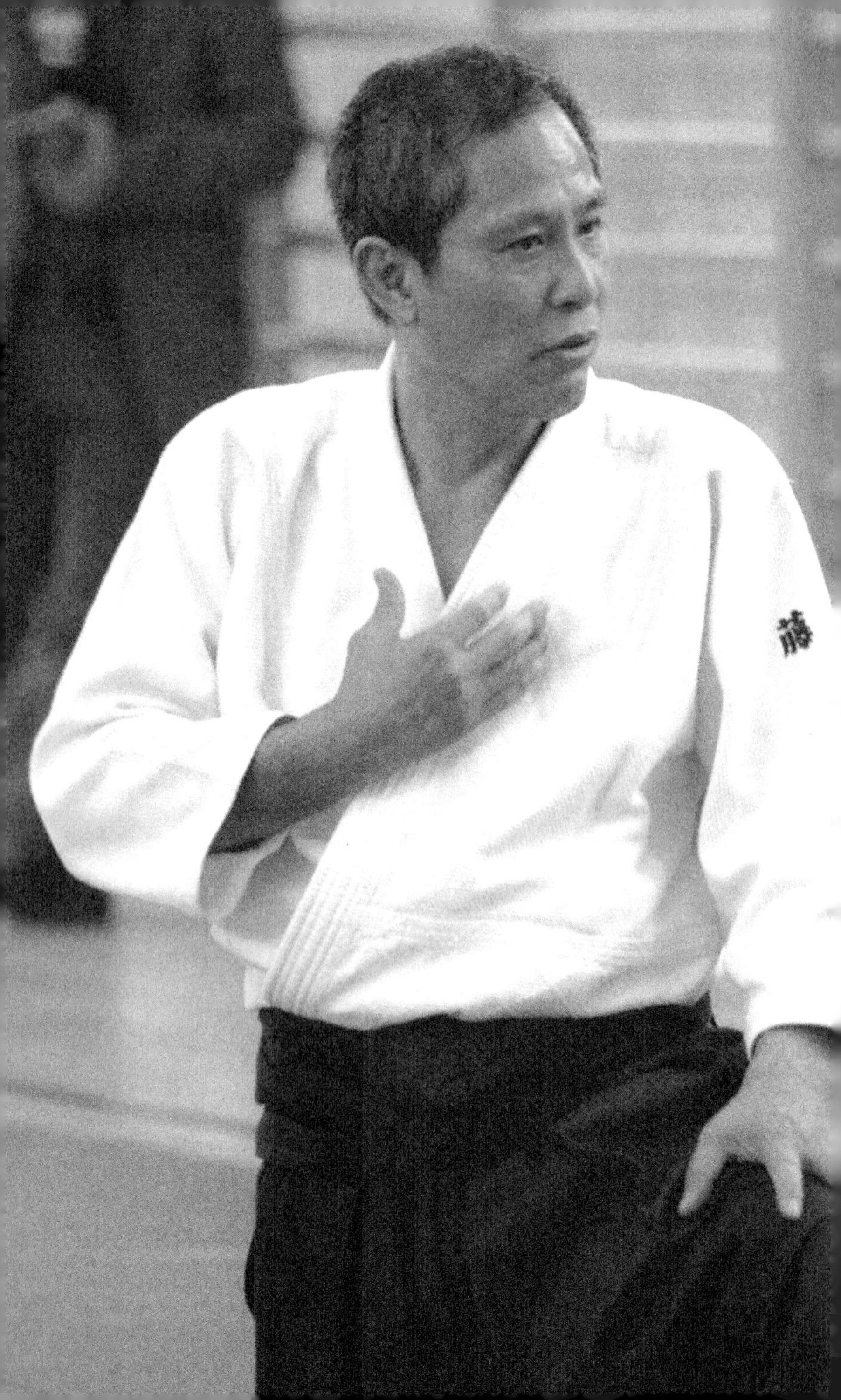
藤

every lesson a novelty.

"Fujimoto, for his part, was tall, at least for a Japanese of his generation; he used wide deplacements, his Aikidō was spiral-shaped, very much in the matrix of the Aikikai Hombu Dojo in the era of the second Doshu, Kisshomaru Ueshiba sensei; he taught in a structured way, very clearly; he had an open personality, he was likeable or at least had a character that could be incredibly pleasant - when it suited him..." [laughs]

"Do you have personal experience of this?" [laughs]

"We are only human. He was extremely pleasant and could be really... [laughs] Never mind. In a way, switching from Hoso to Fuji was like changing organisation, but it happened quite naturally and organically, all things considered, because that was a possibility inherent in our association. For me and the others who followed both, being regularly exposed to this technical diversity was an important step in first preparing ourselves, and then our students, to seek for freedom of expression in our training. Right from the start we realised that training was not a one-size-fits-all affair: as I said before, going to Hosokawa's class meant that he never made you stick to anything, every day there was something that had absolutely nothing to do with that of the day before... sometimes he could drive you crazy, if I'm honest.

"Let's stick to my case and my wanderings. Once I moved to Ireland, I was faced with yet another 'epochal' change, only this time it wasn't my teachers who changed: it was the students. Although all human beings are more or less alike, despite the fact that we all have two legs and two arms and the same joints, in different nations and ethnic groups, there are definite human types. The Irish, generally speaking, are physically very strong, they are very powerful, but also accordingly not very flexible. The average Italian person usually has a more agile and adaptable body, very suitable for *kinonagare* practice. I have wondered many times how much the weather factor has an effect on this.

"When I started teaching in Ireland, I found that I had to change my style of practice again, and certainly not by cultural choice, but rather by necessity. I had to rethink a lot of things because they weren't working for me anymore in the absence of a collaborative uke, and in the presence of a fundamentally more rigid physical type. I was born and raised with an idea of practice based on relaxation, on the agreement between *tori* and uke and on the principle of spherical rotation. I am in no way here to pass judgement on this technical approach, I don't want to say that it is good or bad, but at the time I had to change it, because it didn't work well with the locals. As a 4th dan, in my Irish isolation, I had to dedicate myself to figuring out what it means to study things the way you, Marco, for many years have been doing in Iwama-ryu, i.e. what it means to study *kihon*, to practice from a stationary position, to being held without compromise, etc. I had to find a system to make my new students move and convert them later to practice in spherical rotation. I believe I have done this with some success.

"Years later, in 2009, when I came back to Italy, I had the chance to meet Paolo Corallini sensei, a very fascinating character from both a human and cultural point of view, and then I went to one of his seminars, since I was curious to see how Iwama-ryu was practised. I was amazed, because they did a lot of things I had never seen before, but above all what struck me was that even at first sight it was clear that many of the things I saw could be useful to complement an Aikikai type of practice.

"I was also a little disappointed, because we had never been shown this stuff in our home association. The explanation for this was that we were living in a crazy Aikidō world. Our community was really different, if you look at it through today's eyes. In the time from the early beginnings

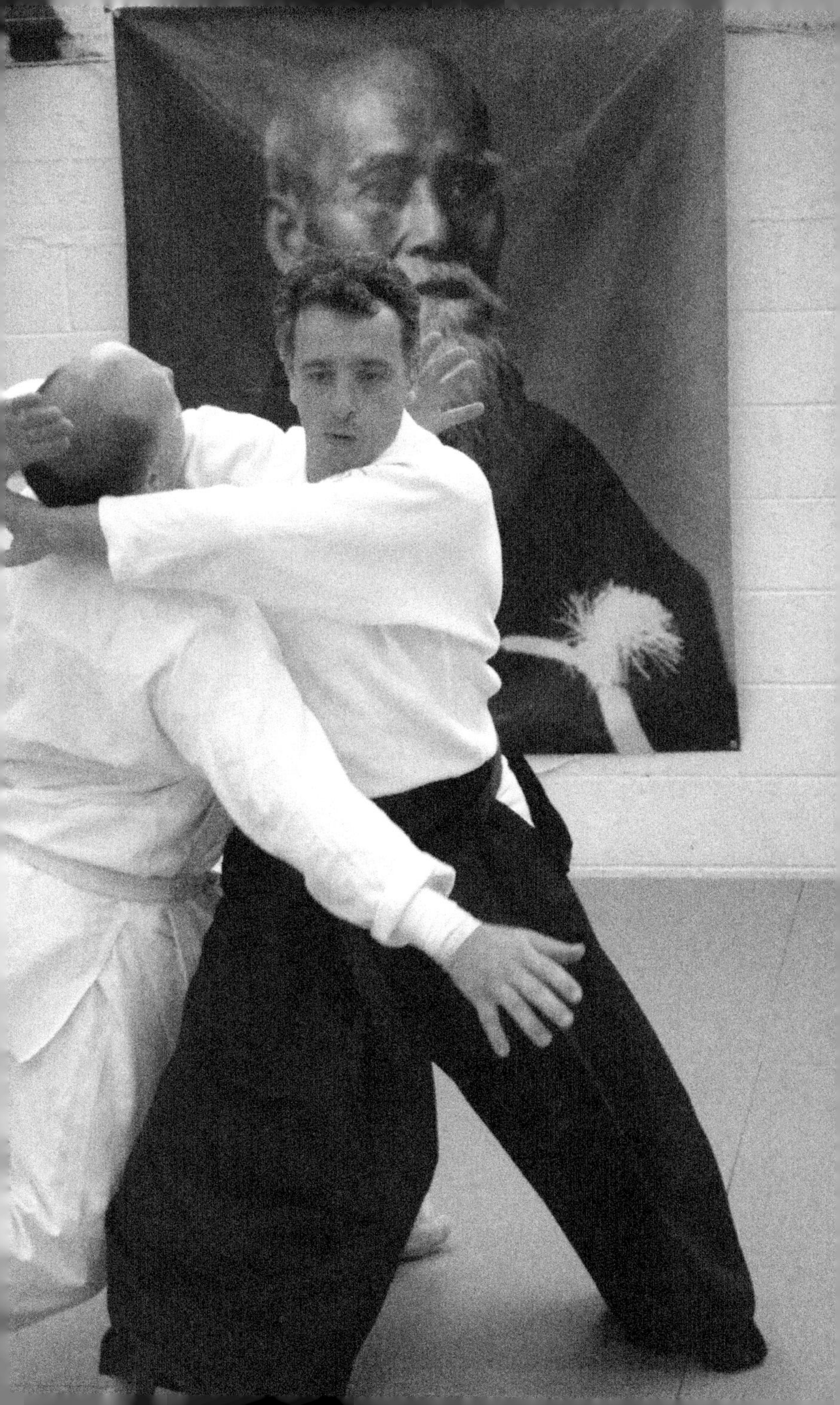

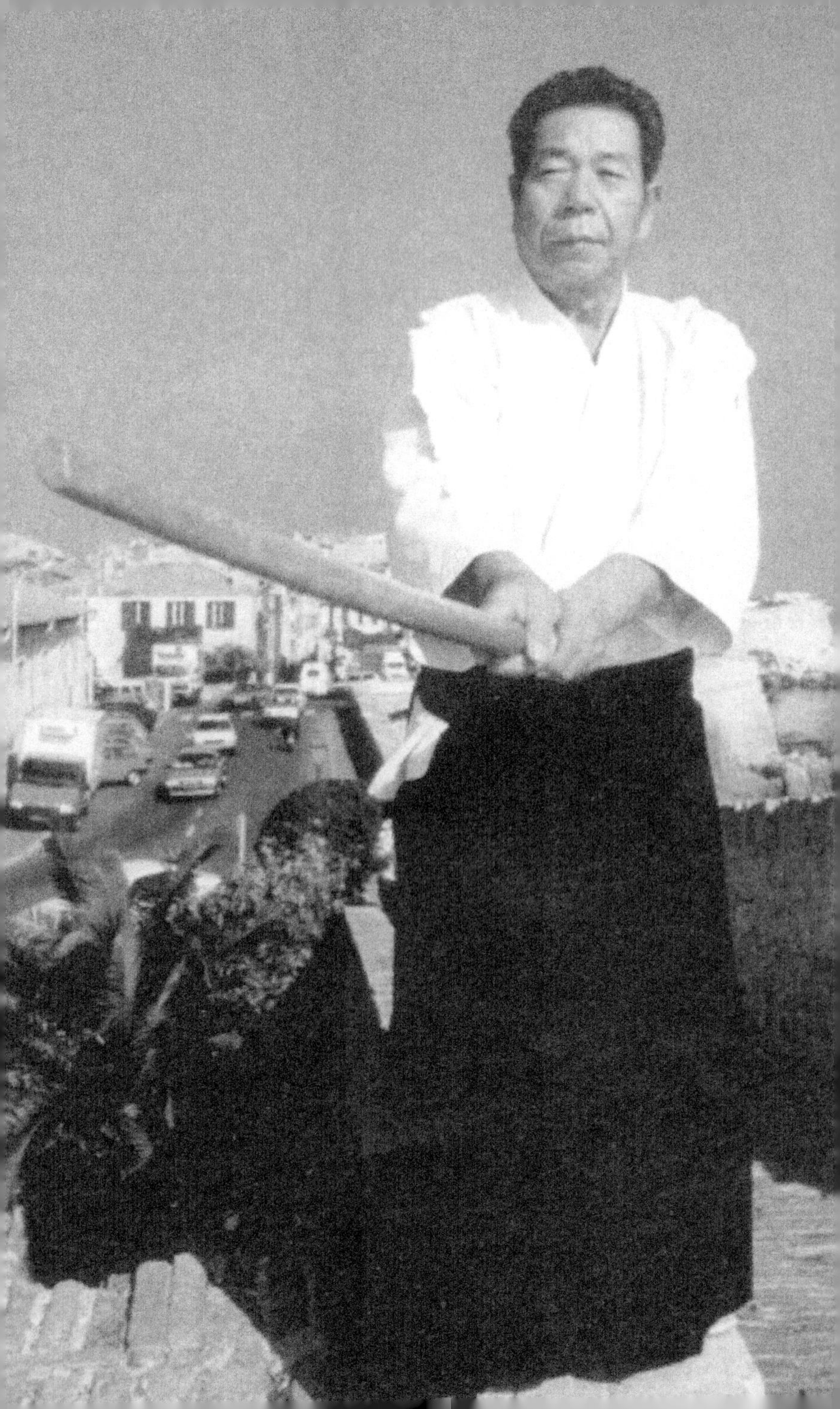

through the 80's, they were all claiming to be sincere aikidōka, in their dōjō they all talked about harmony, peace, hugs, kisses and all that, but the organisations were completely closed. Preposterous things happened, such as when Corallini brought Morihiro Saito sensei to Italy for the first time in 1985: naturally, some of the Italian Aikikai teachers went to attend the seminar, but they all conveniently forgot their Budopass at home, because they did not want Saito's signature to be on it. That booklet was to be presented at seminars and internal exam sessions. Finding Saito sensei's signature on it, instead of being a reason for praise ('Did you see this guy, what a good student, what a keen teacher, how interested in Aikidō, he went to train with Saito too'), could cause serious repercussions.

"This closure towards the outside also had motivations, it was not all negative: nowadays it is easy to criticise, but obviously the Italian Aikikai for a long period of time had been carrying the burden of developing Italian Aikidō almost on its own, and perhaps rightly considered its duty to protect that work. With hindsight we can say that unfortunately it did not have, and it doesn't seem to have to this day, that open-mindedness required to act as a vehicle for the entire community. It has always been, especially from a certain point onwards, an extremely sectorial association and therefore has suffered over the years a myriad of internal splits that continue to this day.

"Time has gone by and over the next thirty years, luckily, the inter-associative climate has markedly changed for the better, although often in spite of the leadership of the various associations, certainly not thanks to them. They simply got swept away by the events. Today anyone can go on the internet, find videos on anyone and information on any event. The variety and quantity of the technical offer have increased out of all proportion, and consequently the opportunities to be exposed to that technical diversity from which one day to draw one's own portion of expressive freedom have also grown exponentially.

"In the past there were many more barriers. Let's go back to the case of Saito sensei's first Italian seminar. How was the event publicised at the time? Just as all the offices of the various organisations used to do on the occasion of an upcoming seminar: someone in Osimo produced photocopied leaflets, put them in a few envelopes and mailed them around, for example to the Dojo Centrale in Rome, to Aikikai Napoli, or to Aikikai Bolzano. Like all other communications, the news of Saito's arrival was then filtered by the various Dojo Managers on the basis of team orders or personal preferences. They did this for years! So: 'Kobayashi, no. Tamura least of all. Tohei, no way, he's a traitor. Asai, yes, because he's my teacher's friend…' It's funny to tell the story today, but that's how it was at the time."

"You know, Simone, it's not even that funny, because in 2015, when together with Fabio Ramazzin I organised for the last time the *Aiki-Census* in Italy, we wrote to all the biggest Italian associations to gain some kind of access to their data (obviously not sensitive), to the figures, because we were trying to get a clear indication of the number of Aikidō students in the various regions, divided by age, district, etc...

"The big associations completely ignored us, because who were we to ask for that information? In reality, you are not talking about something that only concerns the 70's, 80's, 90's and the Italian Aikikai: maybe so, but this mentality is common to much of Aikidō.

"In my opinion, from a certain point of view, what is really making things change now and can make them change even more, is this *[shows a smartphone]*. People who want to know about Aikidō google what Aikidō is. Then they start to get lost in the information and maybe decide to join the dōjō closest to home, because it is the most convenient. However, if the teacher tries to indoctrinate them, like a cult *guru*, 'we

INFORMATION

Nr.: 01/1985
Datum: 24.01.1985

U.I.A
UNIONE ITALIANA AIKIDO

STAGE INTERNAZIONALE DI AIKIDO

TORINO (1-4-5 Febbraio (February) 1985)
OSIMO (AN) (8-9-10 Febbraio (February) 1985)

合気道

DIRETTO DA

HANSHI SAITO MORIHIRO SENSEI

IBARAKI DOJO CHO

AIKI SHRINE (IWAMA)
DISCEPOLO DIRETTO DI O SENSEI
UESHIBA MORIHEI

Società Interpret
Assistant Interprete
Mr STANLEY PRANIN V° Dan Aikido

Nachrichten erbeten an / Please, notify /   Klaus Chudziak, Albert-Sch... Str. 5
S.V.P. Adressez-vous à / Prego di scrivere a: D-6272 Niedernhausen

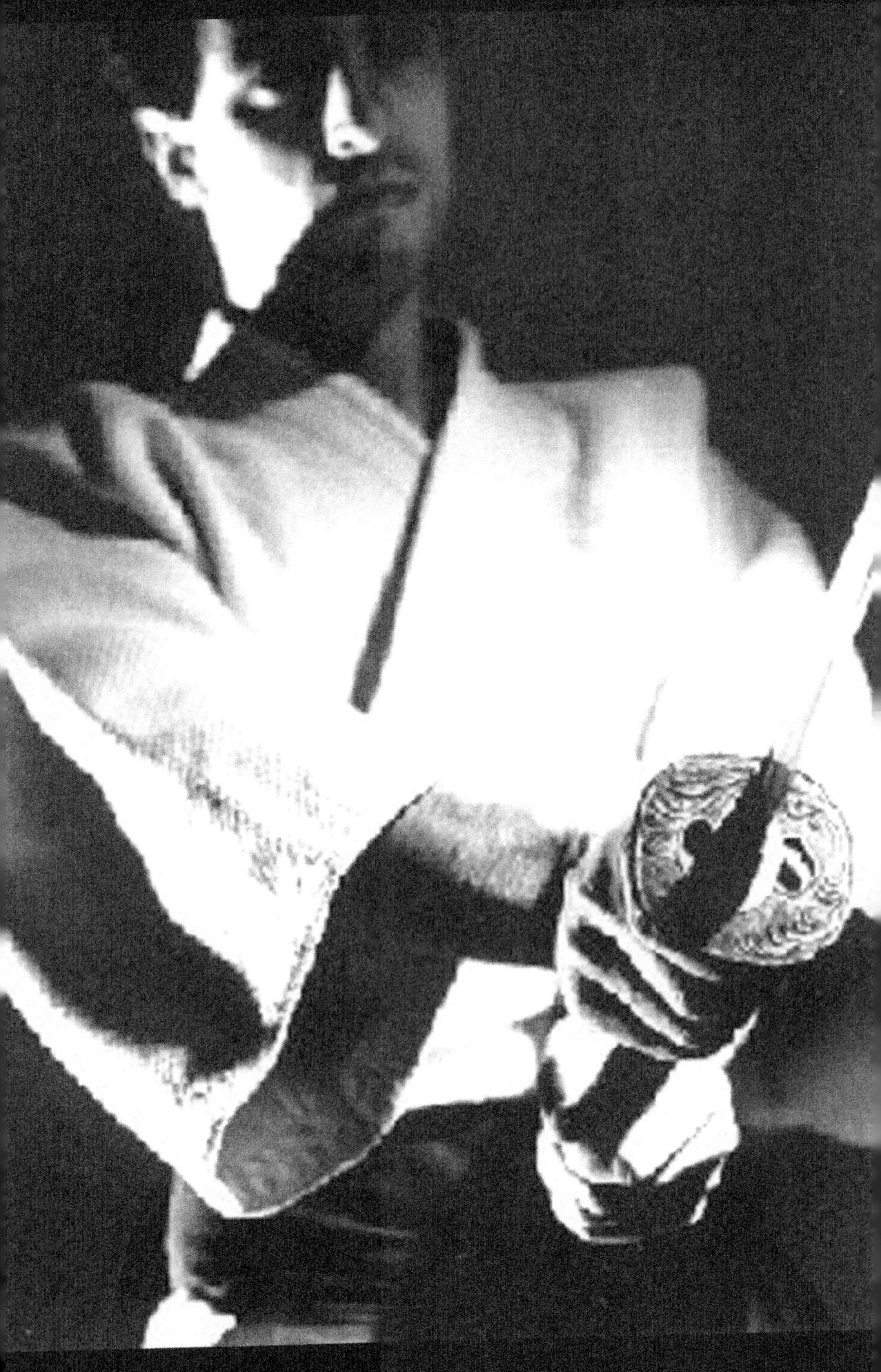

are the best, we are this way, we are that way', I hope that today, a person of a young generation is curious enough to find out what the rest of the world thinks of what the 'guru' is talking about and what else the world has to offer."

"I agree, Marco. This is something that is already happening, but what I hope will happen in the future is that teachers stop with that nasty habit, because it's about time we all admitted that we are simply people on a journey. None of us possess any particular truth. None of our associations, even more so, holds the revealed truth of Budō. Each one of us is on a path: if we had integrity and honesty on the part of those who teach, we could say that 99% of these little problems would not exist.

"Regarding the improved inter-associative relations, perhaps it's also a cosmetic affair: maybe now there are fewer open clashes, but fundamentally the distance has remained.

"Regarding your question, which is what we are fundamentally most interested in, because we are interested in people and not associations, I am convinced that a student needs to have a clear path from X to Y. This is to avoid mix-ups and confusions, and to prevent learning things by halves. From the outset, however, and this ties in with what I have just said, the student should know (and therefore should be told, taught) that there is a plurality of other systems which he should one day experiment with, at least in part. From a certain point onwards, it is absolutely necessary to go elsewhere, and this does not mean denying one's origins and should not translate into having to quarrel with anyone: it is necessary, because otherwise personal development stagnates. We have all been to school, but we have gone from middle school to high school and many also to university. I doubt that in Aikidō one can have a corresponding growth by remaining comfortably always and only within the same style and the same environment.

"I think it is highly advisable that those who have

The Parent

reached a certain level in Aikikai, once they have reached nidan, for example, add a period of training with someone who has studied in Saito sensei's line to their curriculum. In my opinion, continuing to look at things with the same eyes is not an efficient pedagogical solution, that's all. It is not a question of loyalty to schools or having to leave one's teacher: it is not efficient. Getting out of the same box, not necessarily, but probably, could empower you to see those same things from another point of view and find answers in a shorter time, OK? It's all about increasing your learning opportunities.

"I did it in my time and I must say that, going back to my personal experience, that for a while it was not easy. It's not that I suffered, suffering is something else! It was complicated, yes, but I said it myself a few minutes ago: this is Budō, isn't it? Creating situations and then living them. If the situations are always pleasant and enjoyable, I doubt that there is going to be any growth. It was hard, but in any case Corallini sensei supported me constantly, even if I am sure that he sensed from the beginning that I would never remain in Iwama-ryu. With great spirit of service he helped me and taught me what he knew.

"This experience, which I faced when I was already 5th dan, led me to reconsider a number of things. It didn't make me become a new Ueshiba, but I was certainly able to correct two or three points I approached in a profoundly wrong way, because they were pointed out to me by someone who had a different point of view: different from mine, first of all, but also different from my previous teachers. In time, this point of view became mine too, I learned it, so to speak, and then I could re-examine everything else I was doing through this enriched viewpoint.

"For the sake of equality, I would also invite those who have studied in Iwama-ryu to have a complementary experience in a more fluid style; it does not necessarily have to be in Aikikai, it could very well be in Kobayashi-Ryu, for

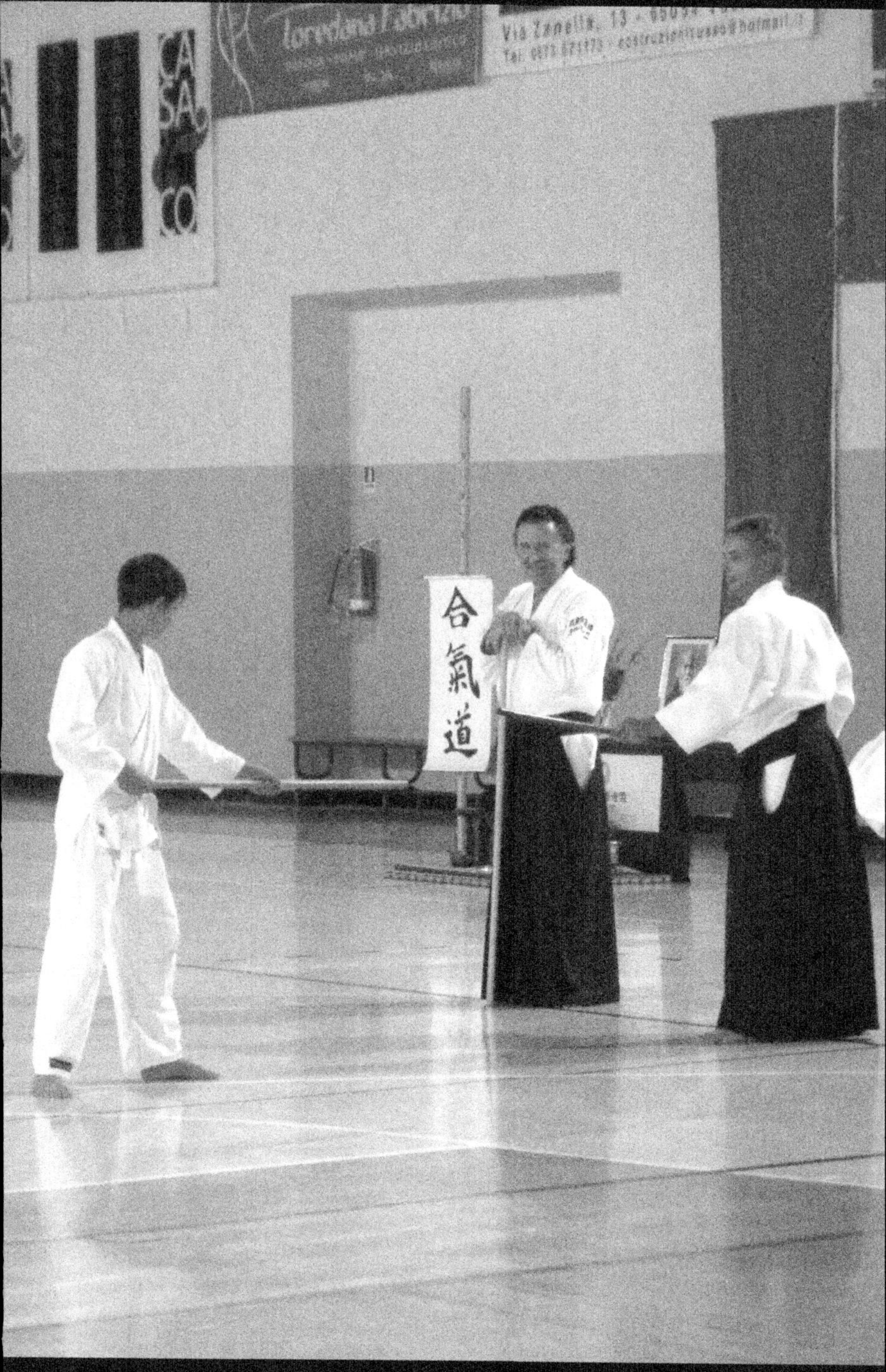
合氣道

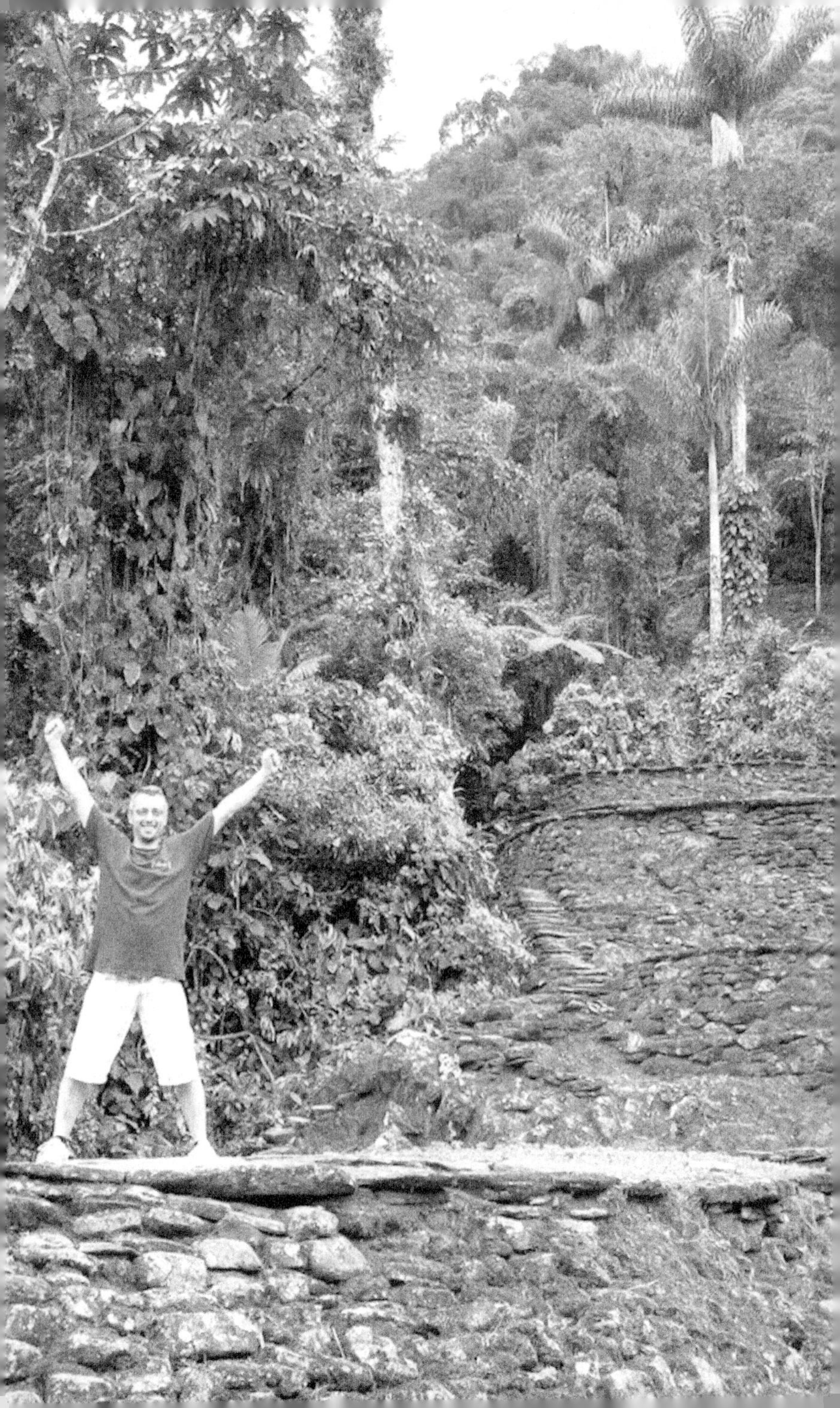

example, or one could go and have a training experience with the Ki-Aikidō group...

"Whoever has been around and practised with the purists of both styles, could easily realise that the former move too much and sometimes in a haphazard way, while the latter move too little and their harmony is more times than not stuck in a sea of patterns, techniques and structures.

"Please bear with me, I would like to conclude what has become a long discussion with a further consideration, which I believe is even more important than what has been said so far: if from a certain point forward it is certainly opportune and necessary to be free within the practice of Aikidō, in the same way, in my opinion, it is also necessary to learn to be free from the practice of Aikidō. I can again tell you a brief anecdote, Marco. Examples are always enlightening.

"This anecdote has as its protagonist an old and dear friend whose name I will not mention - he is now one of the main teachers of the Italian Aikikai. Years ago he told me that every summer for the previous thirty years he attended the two Italian summer seminars of Tada sensei. He told me this because for him this was obviously a reason for pride, and probably from a certain point of view it is too; but on that occasion, and then later on, I always made fun of him for this and said to him: 'Is it possible that in thirty years you have never felt like going to another seminar, with someone else?' Or, also, and here we get to the heart of what I wanted to say, is it possible that you simply don't feel like not doing any summer seminar at all and instead take your rucksack and hat and go, say, to Central America?

"Personally, I have always done it. I have travelled to places that are not normally on the map for ordinary people, because Aikidō has taught me to be curious, or perhaps it is my nature, the two things have merged. I am a bit of a gypsy, as the events I have described to you and my wanderings amply prove. I believe that leaving the active practice of

Aikidō, the one done on the mat, out of our routine (for short periods, I don't mean years, but weeks), helps to develop one's awareness of Aikidō. Again, applying the same principle I described above about going to review my Aikikai Aikidō with new Iwama eyes, an external perspective helps to see better. Even though Aikidō informs 99% of my daily life, being able to see it from the outside, not doing Aikidō, certainly helps me understand it better.

"Incidentally, I have never been one of those mad Japan lovers we often meet in the Budō world. I've been to Japan several times for fairly extended periods and I am interested in some aspects of Japanese culture, but my interests have never been exclusively focused on the East, especially an East like the one we too often experience in martial arts, which is a second-hand or distorted one. I remember talking about this subject with Fujimoto sensei and he told me: 'Look, you people who practice martial arts fundamentally understand very little about Japan, because you are exposed to a kind of Japan and Japanese people that in Japan are very peculiar, because even in Japan martialists are like white flies .'

"Among other things, my background is in classical studies. I was born in Rome and I have always nurtured a very strong interest in our history and indigenous roots. My freedom, and with this I close this long interlude, is also expressed by not always living inside Aikidō and by not staying in a house surrounded by *katana* and *ashi*... To say, rather than *sushi*, I prefer a nice serving of *lasagne*."

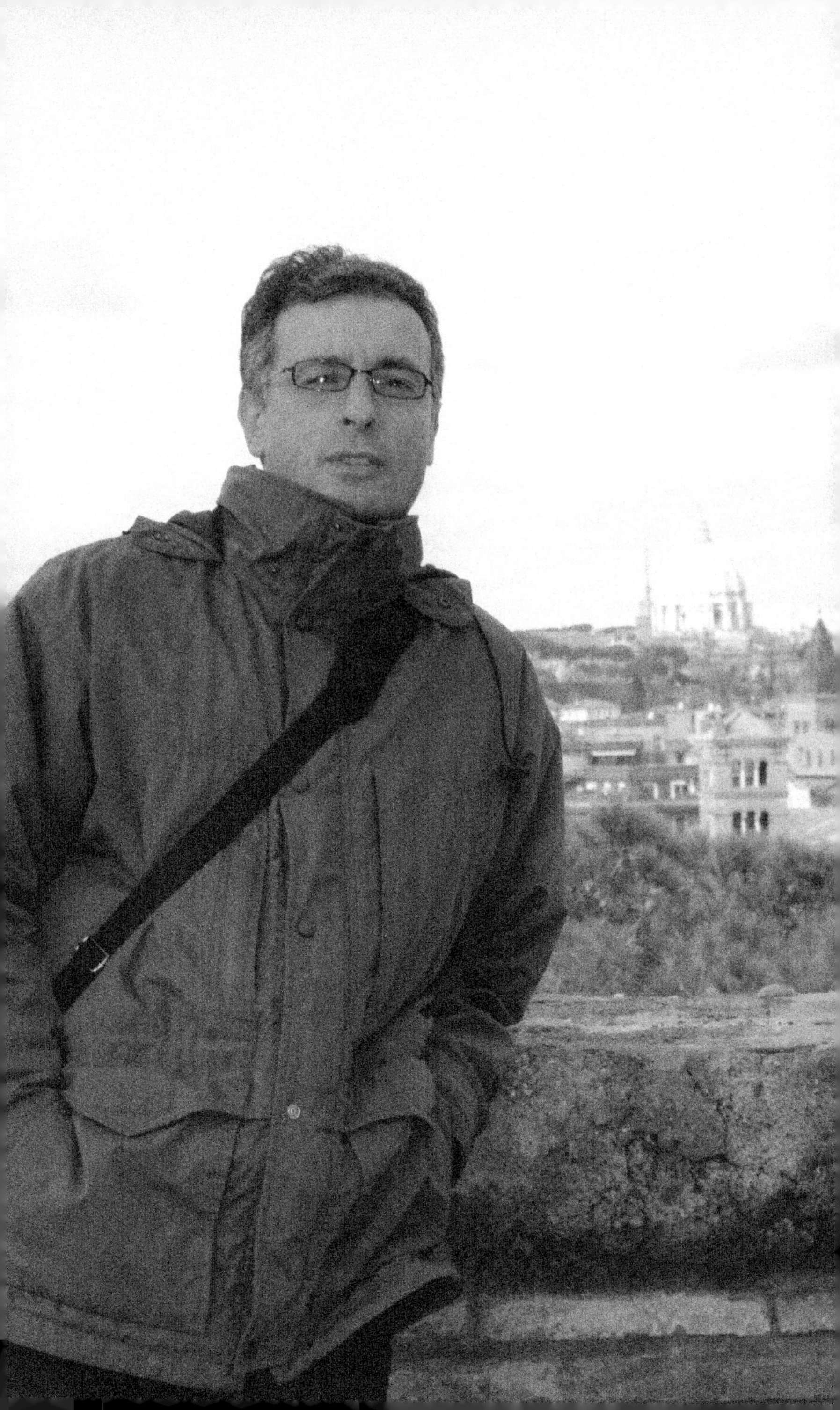

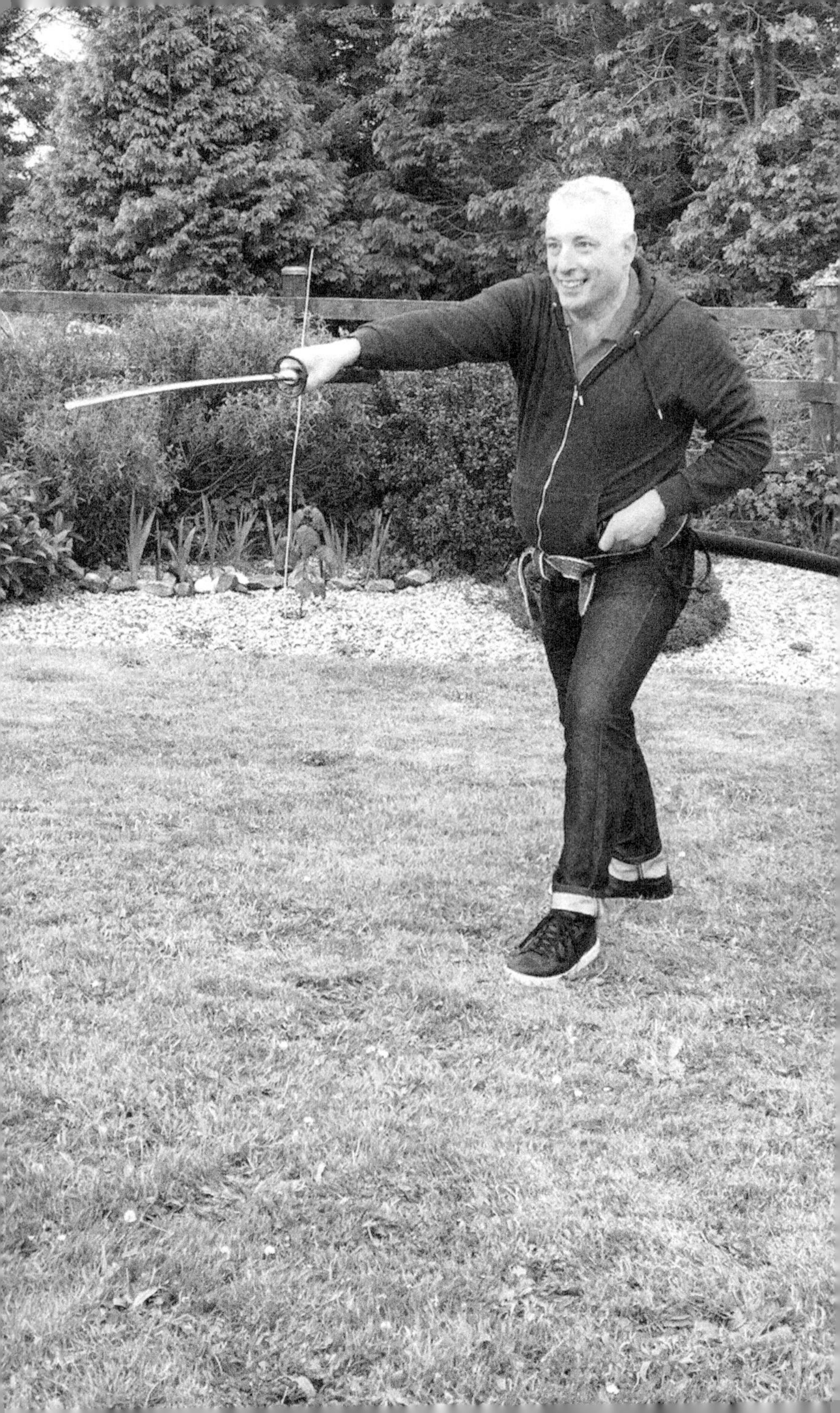

Pandemic Stories

"I would now like to get your feedback on something that I feel is important: how do you see the future of our discipline post-Covid?"

"We have been in this situation for almost two years now, so it is a feeling that has gradually developed within me and my sensations about it have changed. So far, I believe that the consequences of this pandemic (real or alleged) on our civilised society, regardless of what one thinks about its real extent and magnitude, have been very heavy. It will result in a profoundly changed world, and even if we were to return to a completely Covid-free society, I think that many of the habits that have been instilled during this period will persist post-pandemic.

"Regarding Budō, today more than ever, if there was need, we can understand the value of practising Budō as a spiritual path. It is a year that we hear people complain of not being able to practice, but in reality, Marco, who is preventing them? It is only a mental form on the basis of which to do Aikidō you need a dōjō, you need a teacher, you need keikogi, you need companions to practice and so on. You expressed the same concept earlier. This is the prearranged scheme, alright, but excuse me, I must inform you that the game is over and this scheme no longer exists.

"So what do we do? Do we keep complaining and waiting for what may never come back in the form we long for?

"Question number one would be: what is it possible to do? Can one practise alone? Very well, let's practise alone. Can one practise in person with family members? Practise with your family. Can one practise outside without contact? Practise outside without contact. Is it raining? Never mind. Is it snowing? It doesn't matter. Only 4 of the 40 I had before the pandemic came for the above? Be thankful for the 4 who come, it's the 36 people who dropped out that have a problem. Here you can see who practised Aikidō in depth and who was a tourist.

"As I mentioned before, a certain educational model of Budō is designed on receiving both difficulties from the teacher and tools to deal with them. Once one knows how to deal with a certain level of difficulty, the next one presents itself, slowly but steadily increasing. One can assert without fear of being contradicted that without difficulties there is no Aikidō, there is no Budō. Therefore, the pandemic is only a particularly hostile uke that one must deal with, without turning one's back on it. Is it easy? No, certainly not, I'm not suggesting that. A lot of people had family bereavements, it's not easy and it's not desirable, but that's life, and that's what life has thrown at us.

"By the way, to put things in the right proportions, 70 years ago our grandparents enjoyed six years in the company of a war that was the most destructive ever. They came out of it anyway, rolled up their sleeves and the world we find ourselves in today was subsequently born. The Covid-19 crisis, in the end, is only a joke compared to other traumatic events that humanity has repeatedly faced throughout its history, always coming out stronger.

"Coming back to us, as you also mentioned, as far as post-Covid is concerned, the common weakness that

合氣道

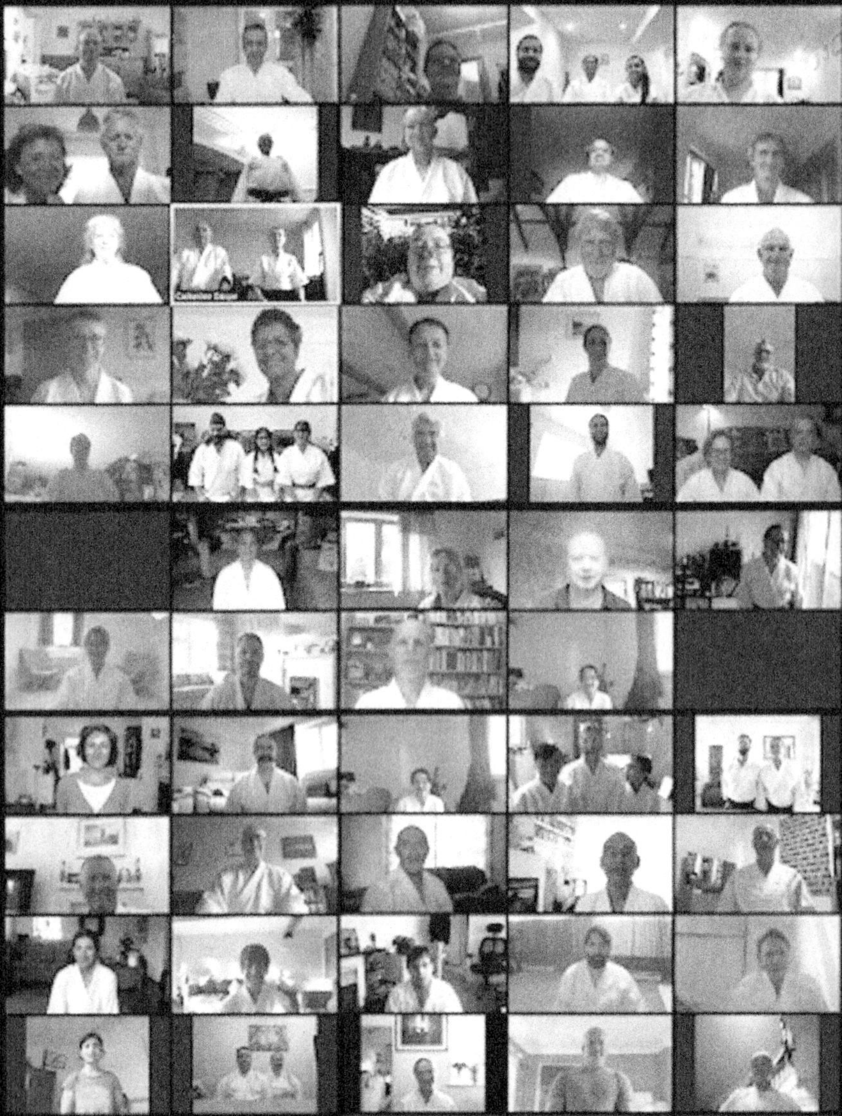

everyone has faced in this period perhaps taught us to abandon that lethal habit of parcelling out practice into styles and stylistic features, thus giving those who run the relevant organisations the opportunity to maintain divisions that are artificial. These divisions do not exist, their only purpose is to maintain the dominant position of those who advocate them.

"Aikidō should be based on solidarity and mutual aid between practitioners: it is necessary to move forward and, little by little, go beyond the perspective in which the single associations exist. In Italy there are already umbrella organisations - you represent one, incidentally - that in the future could interpret the associative model in a freer and more constructive way. The post-Covid (this is my hope rather than a certainty, it is a wish) could perhaps give us this new attitude.

"Another thing: the importance of distance teaching, which today has become a must. At the beginning I think we were all reluctant to use it, because we were prisoners of that scheme I was talking about before: a highly enjoyable scheme by the way, who wants to do Aikidō in front of a monitor? But that was the recent requirement, and this requirement has shown us that the medium can be useful. Therefore it's possible that it will still be used in the future as a complementary training tool. An online class could also serve to attract new audiences of learners belonging to the younger generations and therefore more accustomed to this tool and to the use of visual media in general. If this medium is used within well-defined deontological limits - don't ever tell me about people grading for shodan online, because that's obviously another story - distance learning can be a great resource for Aikidō, and it can be another positive legacy of the pandemic."

"Thank you very much, Simone. By the way, I can only confirm what you're saying: in the class I gave this morning - I'm one of those who have been teaching online every day these days - there was one of my students who moved to Munich, Germany. This is one of the good things about online teaching, it completely removes distance. This morning we studied the variations of the first *kumitachi* and this young man, as well as other people I know, told me: 'Please, when the pandemic ends, let's not stop seeing each other here'. We really owe this opportunity to this out of comfort zone situation, which showed us options we didn't even think existed."

Next page:
Simone Chierchini and Marco Rubatto

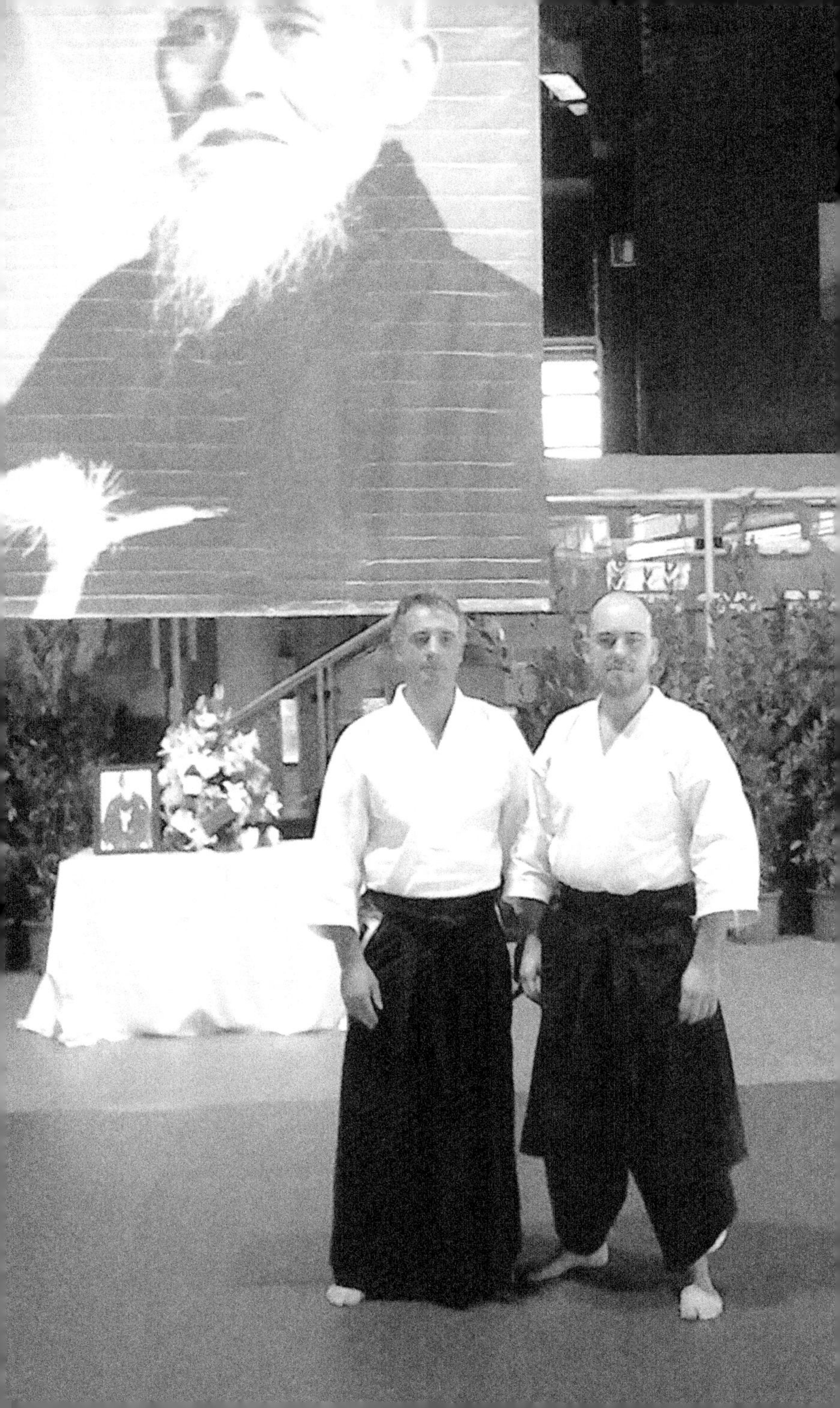

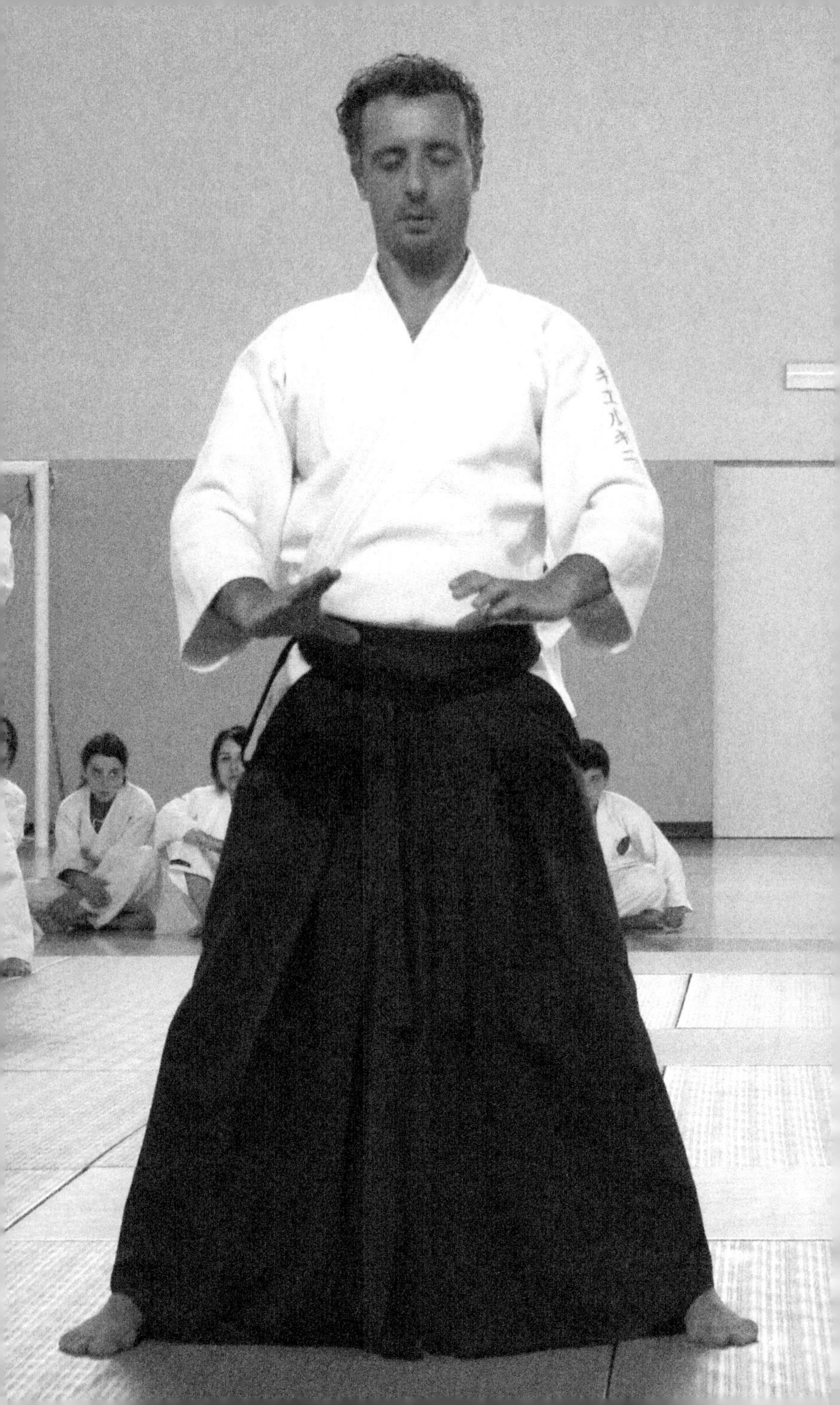

Aikido Italia Network Yesterday, Today & Tomorrow

"Staying on the subject of the web, the last reflection that we would like you to offer us concerns your brainchild, Aikido Italia Network, the channel that is currently hosting us. It is a blog of absolutely remarkable dimensions, both for the content that you and all the people who collaborate with you put online, and also for the high number of users who frequent the site and its associated social media. How do you think this project is evolving? Do you see any shadows or lights?"

"Aikido Italia Network was born as a blog for my personal expression at the end of 2009. It's a bit the same as what happened when I moved to Ireland, I did not have any definite project in mind. I simply wanted to have a container in which I could present the writings I had produced as a journalist and commentator on Aikidō in various national and international publications of this sector since the mid-80s. Back then, having a blog was still a novelty and it was exciting. I liked the idea and I gradually dedicated a lot of energy and attention to it, to the point that in a short time Aikido Italia Network became the centre of my extra-dōjō activities.

"Not long afterwards I started the Aikido Italia

Network group on Facebook, kicking off a season of discussion and debate on the meaning of our practice and its future in Italy. It has been a very interesting and entertaining season: on that Facebook group we have all made plenty of good and bad appearances, but it has certainly taught us all a lot. Thus, it was quite natural that the AIN blog and Facebook Group gradually opened up to experiences and productions that were not just mine. Once I began to speak to the outside world, to communicate, it was natural that I no longer felt it as something exclusively mine, to the point that I decided to include in the blog's name the words 'Libera Comunità di Aikido Italiana' (Free Italian Aikidō Community).

"Over time, then, the blog's path has followed in parallel my technical opening to styles of practice different from the one I started with and with which I later established myself. It facilitated my cultural growth as well, thanks to the stimulating information that flowed into it. This has profoundly modified my vision on the world of Aikidō in general and on the physical dimension of the art in particular.

"Coming to the present day, Aikido Italia Network has in the meantime opened up to a wider public, leaving behind the sometimes narrow confines and limited views of Italian Aikidō, to dialogue with its international counterparts. For some time we have had a beneficial exchange with Chris Li's Aikidō Sangenkai and Ellis Amdur's KogenBudō, for example, and also with other important figures of reference for the diffusion of Aikidō culture in the world, such as Guillaume Erard. We have brought and continue to bring their voices to Italy through authorised translations of their material: it is something that we do formally, I would like to mention, because being an online content creator myself, it has always bothered me that people steal it on the sly left and right. Just ask.

"Aikido Italia Network also has a significant section

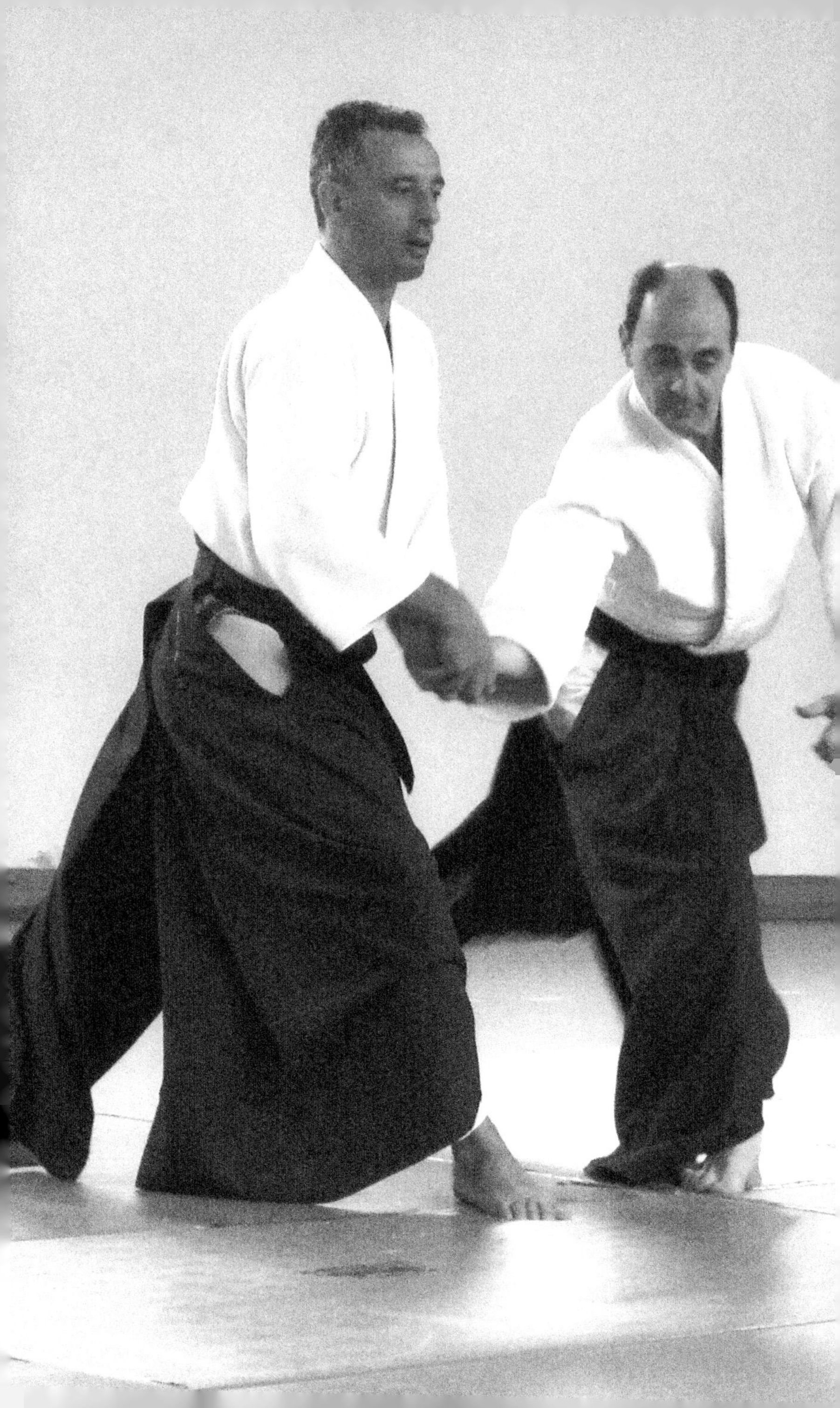

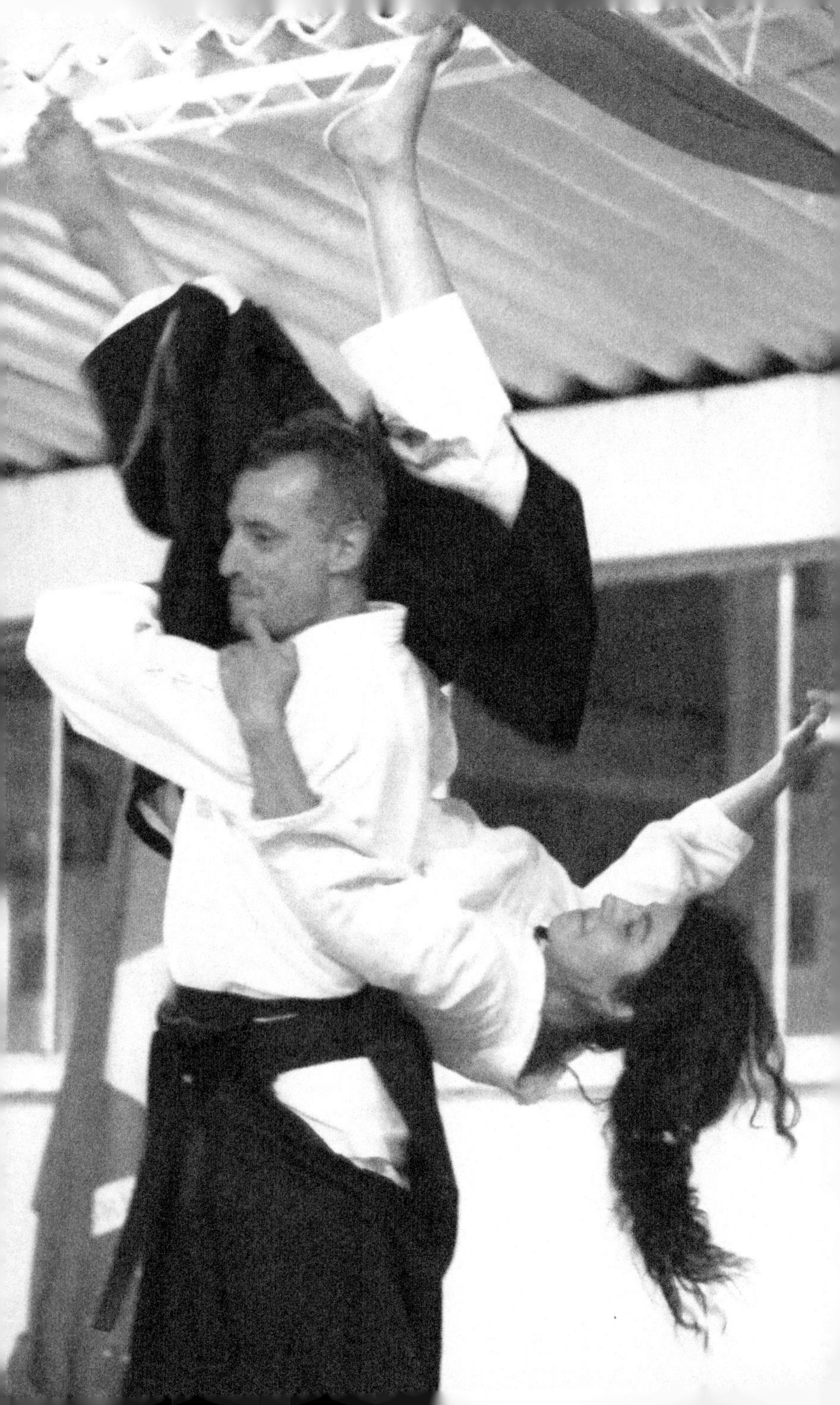

in English, where we strive to bring the best of Italian content production on Budō in English translation, in order to take that excellence we have in our community out of the national borders, that would otherwise remain unheard abroad due to the language barrier. We have done this work with English (within our limits, of course), and at the beginning of 2021 we also started to do some corresponding work in French.

"The pandemic then quite naturally pushed us to move to other media. Aikido Italia Network has had a channel on YouTube for years, but I had never developed it, guilty as charged. Lately it has been growing and last spring it was the recipient of *The Aiki Healings*, a series of live video interviews on Zoom with some of the most relevant personalities in the world of Aikidō today. These interviews helped us cope with the most difficult time of the pandemic and lockdown, with the subsequent forced break from in-person practice.

"While I was talking, I wondered if there were any potential shadows in this project, but frankly, I find it difficult to see any. I deeply identify with it and dedicate a good share of my intellectual energies to it.

"It has also been of great help to me in this period of separation from normal life. Last May, in the midst of the pandemic, Aikido Italia Network launched a brand new initiative: Aikido Italia Network Publishing, the new editorial section of our project. I am very happy and excited about this new initiative, which I hope will bring some good energy to everyone at a time when the future continues to seem uncertain. Although many have declared the death of the printed word, I don't feel that way at all. A paper product has an infinitely higher value than something that is on the web and I am sure that many will appreciate this new opportunity to keep the love for Aikidō alive.

"From a practical point of view, we created two series of small-format books on Aikidō and its people, one in

Italian and one in English. These series come out periodically, a small illustrated volume of about 100 pages once a month, at a low cost, to facilitate dissemination. Our intention is to create a gallery of Aikidō characters, promoting our art and its teachers all over the world. The work is well underway and is receiving much appreciation; we have in the pipeline a whole series of other dialogues with some of the most interesting personalities in our world.

"Finally, another initiative has just been launched and it will run in parallel with the former: we have started a series of Budō classics in translation that are not yet available on the Italian/French market. First was the publication in Italian and French translation of *Dueling with O-sensei*, the classic by Ellis Amdur, with whom we have also agreed on the publication of the Italian version of his other two fundamental works on Budō, *Hidden in Plain Sight* and *Old School*. Exciting times and perspectives lie ahead for Aikido Italia Network and those who sympathise with its shared project."

"Thank you Simone. It is great to see that curiosity and the desire to explore are such a deep-rooted perspective in Aikido Italia Network and in the projects it is carrying out, even in this period. I would say that tough situations are those in which the best ideas come out: historically we have seen that bottlenecks select those who are there from those who are not. In my opinion, Aikido Italia Network is doing an excellent job for our community, for which I think I can thank you on behalf of all those who benefit from the contents that you make available.

"I thank you very much for this beautiful chat, for having told us about yourself, for having offered us your personal vision of the discipline that we all love."

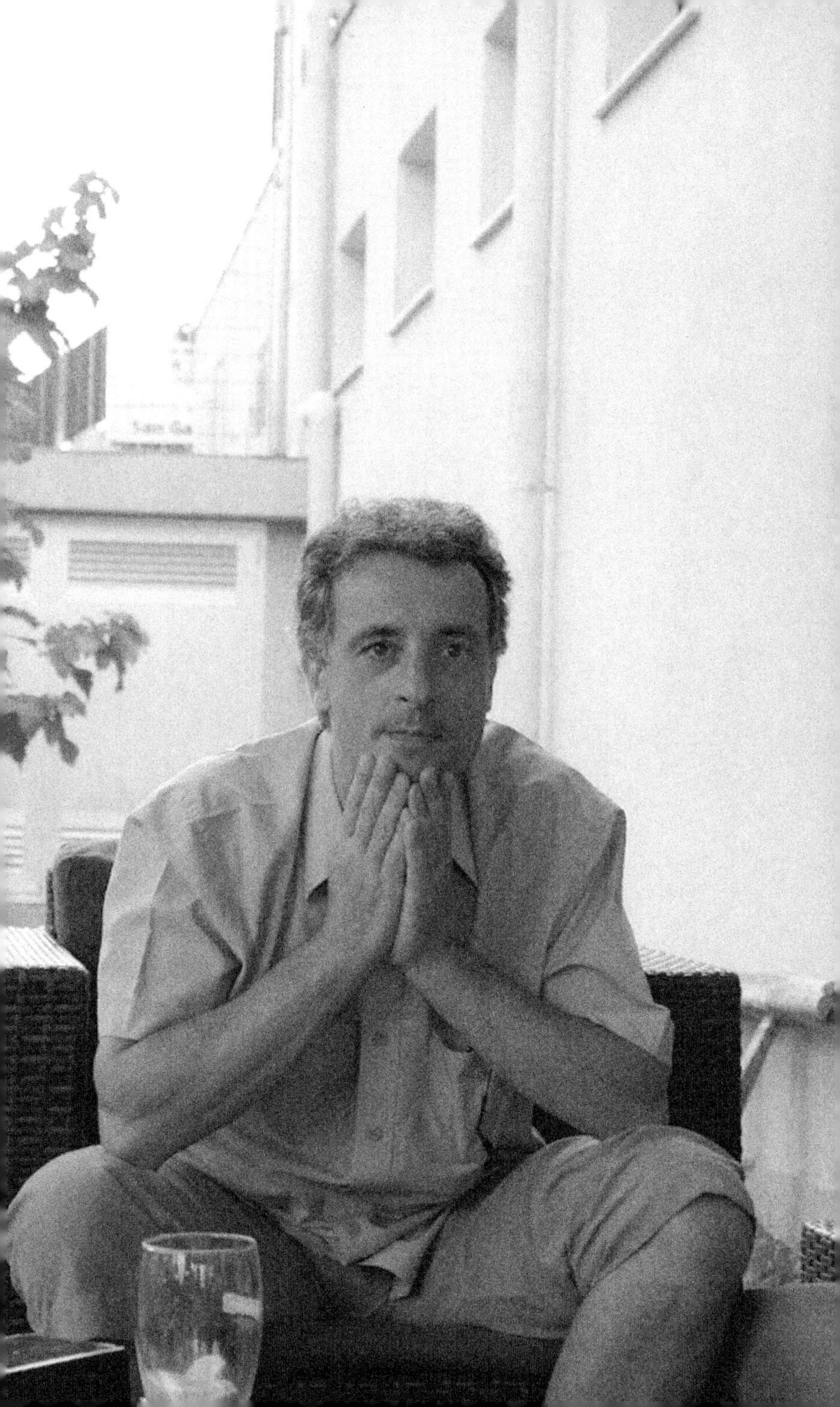

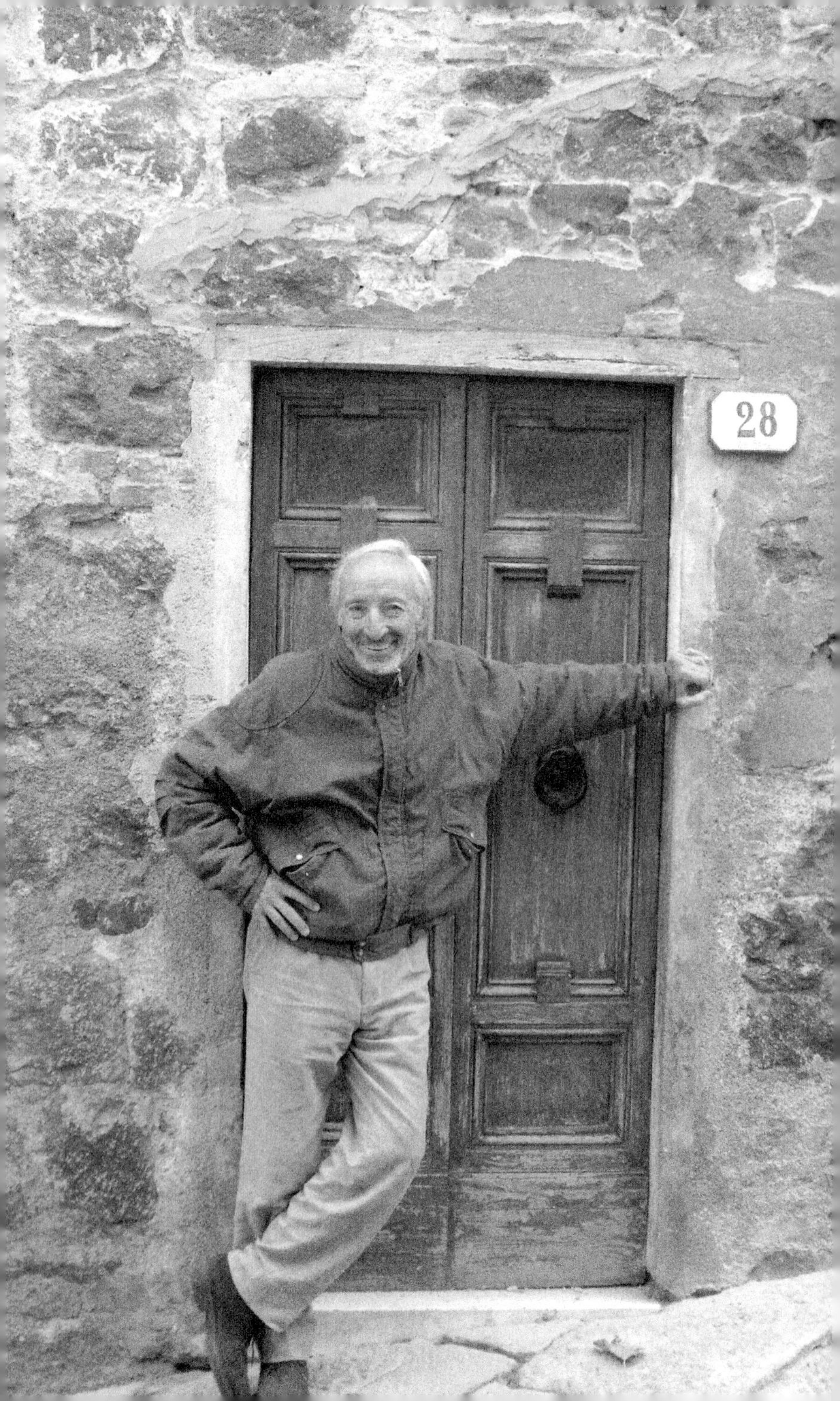
28

Supplement 1
The Great Old Man – Interview with Danilo Chierchini

by Simone Chierchini

Danilo Chierchini is the great old man of martial arts in Italy. A Jūdō pioneer in Italy in the 1950s and a national team champion in 1954; the founder of the first permanent Aikidō dōjō in Italy and the signatory of the letter to the Aikikai Hombu Dojo that brought Hiroshi Tada to Italy in the 1960s; the first Aikikai Aikidō shodan in Italy (together with 18 other pioneers) in 1969; the director of Italian Aikikai Central Dojo in Rome from 1970 to 1993; a founding member and then President of the Italian Aikikai for 12 years; and 5th Dan Aikikai since 1979, he is a pillar of Budō in Italy, even if he has been retired for years and has not been heard from for a while. I tracked him down in his Tuscan retreat, and with the help of some good Vino Nobile di Montepulciano I loosened his tongue. Do not expect, however, the classic interview on Aikidō.

[SC] "Let's start from afar and then move on to what interests us the most. World War II is over and there is a generation of young Italians who have escaped the horrors of war. A world, the old one, has been destroyed and now everything is being redone from scratch, with the influence of thousands of external factors, mainly under the wing of American culture. What are your memories of the post-war period? What was the situation like in Italy at the end of the

1940s?"

[DC] "After the crossing of the front by the allied troops of the Fifth Army, that had incorporated the French colonial army - routed by the Germans at the time and then taken over by the Americans - the Italians were shocked by the 'exploits' of these soldiers, who had distinguished themselves above all for their violence against the civilians and the raping of women. Our liberators, therefore, made a very bad first impression on us. Paradoxically, the Germans, who were occupying my village of Radicofani at the time, being strictly disciplined by their superiors, were under orders not to bother the civilian population in any way, unless of course they were armed or in collusion with the resistance.

"Thus the enemy behaved better with us than the friend: I was 13 years old and I still have this burning memory of meeting the liberators. We listened to Badoglian radio, broadcasting from a sector of Italy that had broken away from the Fascists and regrouped under the king, which portrayed the Americans to us as saviours, the positive energy of the world. On the contrary, on the ground we had the tremendous trauma of seeing that the Germans, that is the enemy, the bad guys, were gentlemen compared to the soldiers of the Fifth Army, who did absolutely all sorts of nasty stuff.

"I could cite a thousand episodes, but this is the reality. Even though I am 82 years old *[in 2011]*, unfortunately I remember certain events as if they had happened yesterday, just as I remember perfectly the bitter disappointment that we all felt. Those who lived on the Adriatic side of Italy did not have to experience our pains, because that part of the front was entrusted to British and Commonwealth troops, whose discipline was perfect, while we who were on the Tyrrhenian side were left at the complete mercy of the liberators, to the point that most

people immediately began to call them invaders.
"Those were very hard times. If it had not been for the tangible help from the United States in the form of hundreds of millions of dollars, I don't know if I would be here talking. The Americans first beat us, humiliated us and sent scum in uniforms to fight on our soil, then, once they had occupied and taken control of the nation, they realised how hungry Italy was: it was populated by legions of barefoot beggars. With the start of the Marshall Plan, an enormous amount of food, provisions and clothing began to fall from the sky. From there, we slowly began to work our way up. I remember I was in middle school at the time and our school had been occupied by evacuees, so we took turns attending classes. The desks were planks on tripods, instead of notebooks we used sheets of newspaper where we wrote on the edges, the lighting was provided by a 25W bulb hanging from a cable on the ceiling. Those were really tough times.
"The Americans put us back on our feet and set us on the road to democracy after 20 years of fascist dictatorship, even if, mind you, it was Italian-style, i.e. watered down. In this, too, we Italians are special: first everyone licked the dictator's backside for twenty years, then they hung him by his feet. Piazzale Loreto episode is one of the darkest in our recent history, in my opinion.
"The recovery from the devastation of the war was incredible. In the space of a few years we went from rubble to an economic boom, accompanied by mass urbanisation. I myself left the Siena countryside, in Tuscany, where my family - a family of small landowners - had lived for generations and moved to Rome. All the social structures that had been commonplace before the war collapsed. Those who worked the land stopped farming, returned the farm's key to the landlord and went to live in the city. All of a sudden the countryside emptied out, something that is still visible today, more than 60 years later. After experiencing hunger, fear and hardship, the Italians enthusiastically threw

themselves into work. This was the basis for our rebirth."

[SC] "In addition to American money, it is not incorrect to say that American values came too, and they replaced the traditional ones at a time when people abandoned everything old: especially since the old principles had resulted in the horrors of war and the misery that came with it."

[DC] "It's not like we had much choice either. That was the feeling of the time: everything Italian, every Italian object was despised and considered inferior, while everyone was running after the novelties coming from the USA."

[SC] "The change in perception was very rapid. In the space of a decade, we were faced with a whole new world, with the consequence that people threw the original furniture of the centuries-old Italian tradition out of the window and replaced it with plastic and Formica. The Italians threw out the bathwater and the baby in it."

[DC] "That's right."

[SC] "After every tragedy there is a season of rebirth and great energy. Your generation has been at the centre of this, in a time characterised by a desire to live, to have fun, to dream and to experiment. Your generation was the first to do things that were previously unheard of in the average population."

[DC] "The reconstruction generation accomplished miracles, working with tireless energy and enthusiasm. This was certainly not for purely patriotic reasons, but because the economy had suddenly changed and even the ordinary man could educate himself, work and earn a good living, something that in the past was precluded to most.

"The Italians were proud to have the power to produce and earn. In the short term, this meant being able to eat their fill and dress elegantly, and then being able to buy a flat in the city, a motorbike or a small car paying in instalments. Tens of thousands of Fiat Topolino were sold, people took to travelling and touring, to savouring the good side of life. Consider that until before the war, the vast majority had never set foot outside the Country and most didn't know what the sea was! In the meantime I had gone to work as a chartered surveyor in Bari, so I bought a Lambretta and used it to make crazy journeys like Bari-Taranto…

"Shortly afterwards I bought a small Rumi motorbike, a 125cc, which was much sought after because it made a strange noise, as if it were a racing car! For my group of Roman friends, the height of bliss was this: starting from the Roman walls at the top of Via Veneto with their unmuffled motorbikes making a hell of a racket and riding down Via Veneto at breakneck speed all the way to Piazza Barberini, risking killing pedestrians and passers-by. Those were other times, we felt and were without limits."

[SC] "Tell us about your on-the-road Rome-Seville trip."

[DC] "In the mid-1950s, some friends and I rented a Fiat 1100 that was hilarious to look at and decided to go and visit Spain. At the time, the country was under Franco's dictatorship and was starving. Spooked by what we were hearing about the conditions in Spain under Franco, we packed our 1100 with spare parts, because if it broke down we wouldn't be able to find them in the Iberian peninsula. Spanish law at the time forbade the import of luxury goods from abroad, and cars were considered as such: Spain's car fleet was made up of antediluvian vehicles.

"The Spain we saw was a wonderful, unspoilt, genuine country. Since we had some money in our pockets, we even took an aeroplane from Barcelona to Palma de Mallorca, which at the time was a very simple fishing village with a spectacular charm. With the fall of Franco and the advent of a new way of thinking and a lot of capital, some of these places became among the most famous spots in European tourism."

[SC] "How did a die-hard non-smoker end up

The Great Old Man – Interview with Danilo Chierchini

working for the State Monopolies Tobacco Factory?"

[DC] "After graduating as a surveyor I won a public competitive examination and on September 1, 1952 I was sent to the Manifattura dei Tabacchi in Bari as a maintenance surveys engineer. I lived in Bari Vecchia, in front of the Swabian Castle. The conditions in the neighbourhood were crazy, it was like being in a third world country... To give an enlightening example, since the houses did not have sanitary facilities, in the morning a small tanker truck would do the rounds of the alleyways, and outside the door of the basements a bucket of sewage would be waiting for the unfortunate workers.

"On the other hand, my rented room was in a wonderful location, with a dream view and the luxury of a proper bathroom and running water. The Bari experience was a turning point for me. I was 20 years old and had some money in my pockets: life was smiling at me. Sometimes at midnight with other friends we would take a boat and go out to sea from the old port. Here we would drop anchor and enjoy swimming and seeing the lights of the famous Bari seafront, pride of the people of Bari. I can still remember them saying in dialect: 'If Paris had the sea, it would be a small Bari'."

[SC] "In all this time did you ever do any active sport?"

[DC] "Never."

[SC] "In the meantime you've arrived in Rome. How did you end up doing Jūdō? How did you get the itch to take up martial arts? What made you interested?"

[DC] "I didn't know anything about martial arts, like the vast majority of people at the time. There were rumours of lethal blows, secret techniques and stuff like that. There was even an advertisement in the newspapers promising, 'The helpless will overcome' and we all laughed like crazy... There were also a lot of charlatans around who had promoted themselves to 30th Dan black belt!"

[SC] "They're still there... At least in this respect things haven't changed."

[DC] "One evening I followed some friends to a Judo club. It was the Kodokan Judo Club in Rome. I stayed to watch and I liked it a lot, because in a world where charlatans ruled, the organiser of this club, which was located near Via Veneto, therefore in a prestigious area, Maurizio Genolini sensei, was a true and sincere Jūdō enthusiast. I enrolled and started practising with enthusiasm.

"After two or three years it almost became a problem for me, because practising a competitive martial art at the age of twenty plus was not easy: I was already 'too old'. It was at that time that I happened to see a TV documentary shown on the Italian state broadcaster about a strange art called Aikidō. This programme was based on the exploits of the art's founder, O-sensei Ueshiba. It proceeded to explain that his family had inherited particular techniques, dating back to the samurai era, which were passed down from father to son and not taught to anyone. What I saw struck me deeply and aroused my curiosity. However, I could not find anyone who could teach me this discipline."

[SC] "Was there nobody teaching it in Rome?"

[DC] "There was no one teaching it in Europe, with the exception of France. Around the same time, I learned that a Japanese student had arrived in Rome, a young man who had won a sculpture scholarship from Rome's Academy of Fine Arts. His name was Ken Otani and he was an amateur Jūdō graduate. Genolini immediately appointed Otani as technical director of our Jūdō dōjō. This was the beginning of a training relationship that lasted for several years, but the most remarkable and satisfying thing for me was that under Otani sensei's guidance - despite the fact that I had started Jūdō late and my body wasn't really suited to the discipline - after three years of training we managed to win the Italian team championships. In this team I was the lightweight. That was in 1954: it was one of the greatest joys I had from practising martial arts.

[SC] "After practising for several years at the Kodokan Judo Club with Otani, through your work you had the opportunity to open your own Jūdō dōjō as part of the State Monopolies recreational club in Rome."

[DC] "Over the years I had the opportunity to

advance in rank and I felt like teaching. Given that the State Monopolies had some premises that were closed and practically abandoned, which I was aware of, as I was part of the Maintenance Office, by dint of insistence we managed to convince the management to turn them into a martial arts hall. We carried out the restoration works and opened a beautiful dōjō in the heart of Rome, in Trastevere. This dōjō, which began as a Jūdō school, would later host the first organised and permanent Aikidō class in the history of the discipline in Italy. Until then, the development of Aikidō in Italy had been limited to the sporadic appearance of a few Japanese teachers for seminars of a day or two as guests of other martial art clubs. The students that attended those seminars were jūdōka and karateka curious to try a new discipline, but with no plans to establish the art and teach it on a regular and consistent basis. Our classes, on the other hand, were permanent and established with the idea of spreading Aikidō in Rome."

[SC] "Did you meet Haru Onoda, one of these pre-Monopoli pioneers, before or after you met your first Aikidō teacher, Motokage Kawamukai?"

[DC] "I met these two pioneers more or less at the same time, between the end of 1963 and the beginning of 1964. At that time Kawamukai was an 18-year-old lad who had already had some experience of teaching Aikidō in the United States. He had been responsible for starting Aikidō in New York in collaboration with an Italian-American and an American, Oscar Ratti and Adele Westbrook, who would later become famous for the book they wrote, *Aikido and the Dynamic Sphere*. At a certain point their relationship fell apart and Kawamukai decided to move to Rome, where he had the contact of an old martial arts enthusiast, Tommaso Betti Berutto, the author of a manual on martial arts that was very popular back then.

"Betti, on being contacted by Kawamukai, advised him to get in touch with me, since we had one of the most beautiful dōjō in Rome, and Kawamukai phoned me. It was very late at night and he spoke in English, which we both knew but not too well, nevertheless we managed to understand each other and arranged an appointment for the following days. When I met Kawamukai, I was faced with a young man with great willpower and determination. He wanted to practice Aikidō in Rome, and offered me on a silver platter the opportunity to practice that discipline which I had only seen in that TV documentary, but which had really fascinated me. Within a few days we decided to include an Aikidō class directed by him within the activities of the Monopoli Dojo in Trastevere, and from there the Aikidō movement in Italy took off."

[SC] "Have you ever hosted Haru Onoda at the State Monopolies? This pioneer of Aikidō in Italy was living in Rome at the time, after having been O-sensei's secretary."

[DC] "Onoda didn't teach but she often came to train. She was a young and frail lady who lived in Rome for the same reasons as Ken Otani: she was studying at the Academy of Fine Arts after winning a scholarship. Onoda probably had wanted to teach too, which brought her into conflict with Kawamukai, so we ended up not seeing her anymore.
"From among my teachers over many decades in Budō, the one I remember the most fondly and respectfully remains Ken Otani, with whom I developed a true friendship. Otani was a rather peculiar guy, at least in the eyes of the ordinary Italian person of the time, and the anecdotes he told me were truly fascinating. For example, like all his classmates at the Meiji University in Tokyo, at the outbreak of World War II he enlisted in the air forces and was therefore a pilot. He used to tell me that for them the use of a parachute was inconceivable. The very idea of going into battle with a device that would allow them to jump and abandon the fight was simply an abomination, a disgrace. Each of them was

ready to sacrifice his life for his country, this concept was commonplace, unquestioned and comfortably embraced. Their plane was equipped with a parachute, but they would pull it out of its container and sit on it like a pillow, because it was soft and comfortable...

"Otani was on the list of pilots assigned to suicide missions, and he had trained as a *kamikaze*. He was only saved because the Japanese nation collapsed a few days before his turn came. My friendship with Ken Otani was something I will never forget, as well as his compassion and kindness: he never made me feel that he was the teacher and I was the student. It was through Otani that I came to know and appreciate the Japanese mentality of the time, which was characterised by a number of principles that for me were and have remained essential: keeping one's word, being honest, following the rules one has set for oneself... in a nutshell, the exact opposite of what we see in the behaviour typical of so many Italians. Otani was the teacher who paved the way for me to understand *Bushido* through his personal behaviour."

[SC] "How did it happen that you and Kawamukai wrote to the Aikikai Hombu Dojo requesting a resident teacher and they sent you Hiroshi Tada?"

[DC] "At that time Kawamukai had neither the age nor the science to become the driving force behind the diffusion of Aikidō in Italy, and moreover he had other personal projects in mind besides martial arts. It was he who told me that it was necessary to bring in a professional teacher from Tokyo, and he worked through the contacts he had with Hirokazu Kobayashi - whom we had hosted in 1964 for a seminar at the dōjō - to try and accomplish this ambitious project. Oddly enough, he got it right, because Tada sensei had wanted to come and teach in the West, as Tamura and Yamada had done that very same year. He therefore accepted our invitation and arrived in Italy on

October 26, 1964. Who knows why he did such a thing? Perhaps he was looking for a change in his lifestyle, to test and prove himself in a country completely different from his own in terms of both mindset and culture. Tada sensei's decision to come, this act of courage, has always given me pause. There is no doubt that the Japanese of that time were truly people to be reckoned with."

[SC] "Tada sensei therefore began teaching Aikidō in Italy in your dōjō in Trastevere."

[DC] "Yes, that's right. I used to pick him up in my car from the accommodation I had found for him and escort him around Rome. In those days we trained for two hours three times a week. I used my contacts in the Judo Federation and we organised demonstrations, including one in 1965 that went down in the annals: the demo at the Police Academy in Nettuno. We took the mats to a forecourt within the barracks and had several hundred would-be police officers around as spectators. Tada made an impressive demonstration with Kawamukai and I as uke and was a great success among those present."

[SC] "Who do you remember among the aikidoists of the day?"

[DC] "A first group of enthusiasts was forming. Among them I remember Brunello Esposito from Naples, Nunzio Sabatino from Salerno, Fausto De Compadri, Francesco Lusvardi and Giorgio Veneri in Mantua, Claudio Bosello in Milan, and Claudio Pipitone in Turin. Thanks to this first group, Aikidō took its first steps, to the point that we were able to invite a second Japanese instructor to take care of the south of Italy, Masatomi Ikeda."

[SC] "What memories do you have of the first

Aikikai Dan grading session held in Italy?"

[DC] "The first group of Italian aikidoists to receive Aikikai Hombu Dojo certification was quite large. The exams were held by Tada sensei at various venues during the 1968-69 training year and qualified the first nineteen Italian Aikidō yudansha: Bosello Claudio (Milan), Burkhard Bea (Naples), Chierchini Carla (Rome), Chierchini Danilo (Rome), Cesaratto Gianni (Rome), De Compadri Fausto (Mantua), De Giorgio Sergio (Rome), Della Rocca Vito (Salerno), Esposito Brunello (Naples), Immormino Ladislao (Turin), Infranzi Attilio (Cava dei Tirreni), Lusvardi Francesco (Mantova), Macaluso Marisa (Mantova), Peduzzi Alessandro (Milano), Pipitone Claudio (Torino), Ravieli Alfredo (Roma), Sabatino Nunzio (Napoli), Sciarelli Guglielmo (Napoli), Veneri Giorgio (Mantova).

"At the time, the exams were very tough, or at least we thought so. I personally remember it as a massacre: Tada was really serious about it and didn't make exceptions for anyone."

[SC] "There is an urban legend around that in those early years Tada sensei was very rough in his practice. Is that true?"

[DC] "Absolutely not. On the contrary, it was the Italians who were hard, as hard as rocks, because they thought they had already become some sort of Aikidō champions... Tada sensei was truly gifted with remarkable energy and if he had wanted to play the bad guy he could have broken two or three beginners every night, but obviously he was careful not to do that, since he was trying with extreme hard work to build up his school."

[SC] "In this initial stage, you received the first approaches from the Italian National Olympic Committee (CONI) with regard to integrating Aikidō among the disciplines governed at national level, by forming a national federation recognised by the state. Why was it decided to keep the Italian Aikikai out of CONI? This decision turned out to be a momentous one, in the long run, because there lies the seed of what we see today: after almost 50 years there is no national Aikidō diploma in Italy, no federation recognised by the state, etc. How did this happen and why?"

[DC] "Attempts were made in that direction, which also led to a discussion table to take the project forward. However, every attempt to reach an agreement came up against the fact that the management of the entire movement would have to pass to CONI through the then Italian Federation of Heavy Athletics. For Tada sensei this solution was simply inconceivable. The idea was that the Ueshiba family owned a kind of patent, an invention. The shihan sent to spread the teachings of the Ueshiba family were not prepared to make any compromises. Things like federations, democratic associations, elections of representatives were - at the time - totally alien in relation to the culture and the way of acting of the Japanese instructors dispatched to the West from the Aikikai Hombu Dojo. Zero, not even something to speak of.

"According to Italian law, a state of affairs managed the Japanese way was precluded. We were therefore caught between the inability to combine the democratic system, prescribed by law and proposed by CONI, with the pyramidal management system typical of traditional martial arts. Thus it was decided to proceed autonomously from CONI, in order to protect Tada sensei's work and, at the same time, give our association a legal form that would be acceptable under Italian law. This was the immense work of a long-dead friend, Giacomo Paudice, a lawyer who dedicated years of effort to this project. With my modest contribution we devised a ploy which consisted in setting ourselves up as an association for the promotion of traditional Japanese culture, of which the Italian Aikikai was a section. As a cultural discipline, and not a sport, we broke away from CONI and left their sphere of influence, which is limited to sporting activities. In fact, in 1978 we received recognition as a Moral Body on the proposal of the Ministry of Culture."

[SC] "Since we are already rummaging through the family's dirty laundry, let's try to shed some light on another extremely controversial point in the history of Italian Aikidō. How did it happen that all the Aikidō seniors who did not conform with the Tada line were excluded from the Italian Aikikai or prevented from participating with equal dignity in the life of the association? This is another of the seeds of the troubles that still plague our dysfunctional community decades later. How is it that this association, which managed to establish itself through its own resources and enjoyed the charisma of one of the world's greatest Aikidō teachers, was unable to manage the Italian Aikidō movement in its entirety? From the very beginning, the Italian Aikikai's policy was to exclude those who did not conform, a policy which was then made clear and consolidated with the periodical purge of all those elements which disturbed this conformity. Where does this attitude come from?"

[DC] "It's not that I like what you said, but I think it's almost inevitable. Where there are great leaders, there are great interests. Even on a smaller scale, this phenomenon occurs exactly the same, with jealousies and envies that are all the greater the smaller the technical and moral understanding of the discipline may be. Honestly, as president and administrator of the Italian Aikikai I have not been able to remedy all that has happened, and even now I cannot imagine what I could have done to avoid it. I had the misfortune to be the president of the Italian Aikikai for several years, and I lost friends, time and money because of these problems. Managing the association's meetings has put me at risk of a heart attack on more than one occasion."

[SC] "Is it therefore accurate to say that gradually the handling of Aikidō management and its politics have killed your enjoyment of practising Aikidō?"

[DC] "Perhaps. However, I want to make it clear that I have never cared at all about being president, about managing, about all that paperwork. Those who know me are aware that I'm an elusive individual who hates being in the front row. However, with modesty, at a certain point in the history of the Italian Aikidō community, I was one of the few who had the human and cultural qualities to bear the burden of management, and this burden was imposed on me by others, starting with my teachers. So it turned out that I had to deal on a daily basis with the bureaucracy needed to run an association of several thousand members in a country like Italy. I did this for years, neglecting my family, and without receiving many thanks, neither from the colleagues nor from my teachers. I even had to listen to people talking behind my back, suggesting that I benefited financially from running the organisation, when on more than one occasion I plugged its holes using my own bank account. Then one day I had enough, and I broke from Aikidō politics as much as from Aikidō."

[SC] "After 25 years without martial arts, at the age of 82, are you better or worse off?"

[DC] "I think there is a season for everything. There is a time when you do certain things and you enjoy doing them, and times - as the years go by - that this perspective changes. Goals change, perceptions change. I have never liked chatting. As a jūdōka I was a competitor, not a Jūdō historian. In Aikidō I was part of the pioneer generation, with all the enthusiasm and energy that this entailed. I have been in Aikidō for almost 30 years, and it is normal that my perception has changed. One day, when I realised that I didn't like what I was doing any more, I simply said 'No more'. My greatest satisfaction remains the fact that even today, wherever I go, I meet former students who show me their affection and gratitude for what we shared. I am proud of my reputation in the community, as in other activities of my life. Reputation is something we shine by our actions on a daily basis; after that we can safely go our separate ways, ignoring the squeaking rats that infest all things human."

[SC] "Would you step on the mat again?"

[DC] "Never."

[SC] "Never say never?"

[DC] "If I stepped onto the mat today, I'd only do it to say or listen to a lot of talk. Instead, one should step onto the tatami the way Ken Otani told me the old Japanese used to: they would arrive, throw their clothes on the ground in a corner, put on their keikogi, jump onto the mat, bow to the first person who came along, give each other a good thrashing, get dressed and leave. That's how I see it, the rest is all chatter."

Copyright Simone Chierchini ©2011
All rights are reserved

*Danilo and Simone Chierchini
in front of Radicofani's Fortress*

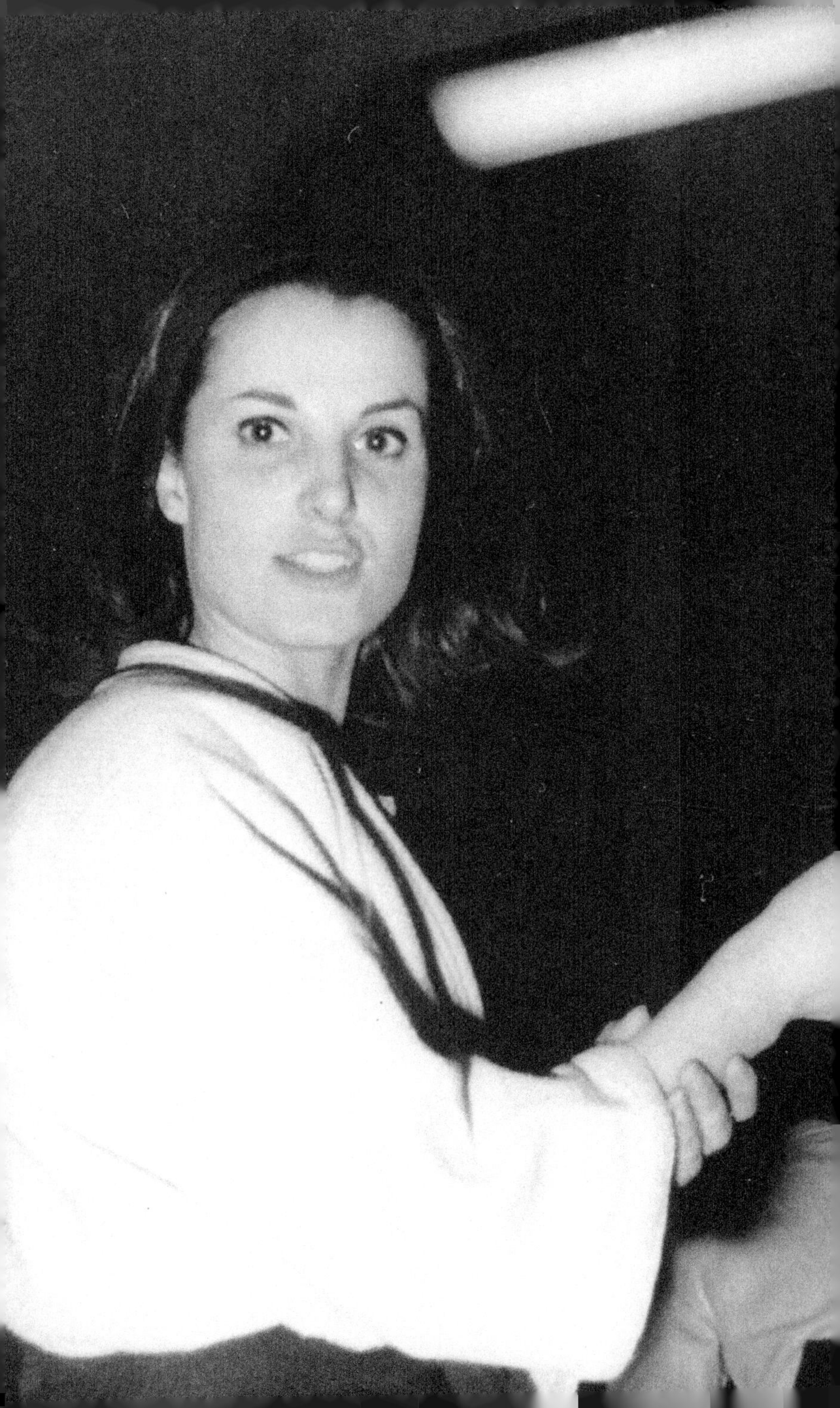

Supplement 2
The Lioness
Interview with Carla Simoncini

by Simone Chierchini

On the occasion of Aikido Italia Network's tenth anniversary [January 2021], we have realised the following interview with Carla Simoncini, a pioneer of Italian Aikidō. Carla was part of the first group of Aikidō enthusiasts that in 1969 received the Aikikai shodan from Tada sensei. She was the female protagonist of an unforgettable time in terms of enthusiasm and energy in the development of the art in Italy.

[SC] "Hello everyone, good to have you back. Today is a special occasion: Aikido Italia Network celebrates its 10th birthday. We have become old! For this occasion we have the unique opportunity to discuss with a pioneer of Italian Aikidō: Carla Simoncini was among the very first to practice the art in Italy, probably one of the first women if not the first one altogether - difficult to know with certainty, given the lack of documentation.

"Carla began Aikidō in 1964 in Rome at the Monopoli Dojo under the guidance of Motokage Kawamukai sensei. Following the arrival of Hiroshi Tada sensei - we are talking about October '64 - her teacher became Tada sensei, whom she followed for a number of years and therefore had a more unique than rare opportunity to be his direct female student in a special time for Italian

Aikidō: the magical Aikidō of the beginnings.
"Incidentally, guys, Carla Simoncini is my mother. So am I pardoned for calling her mum?"

[CS] "Good evening to you and to the people following this interview who, like me, have had or have this special martial art in their hearts."

[SC] "This is a conversation that we have been meaning to have for years - and have never actually managed. I think that Aikido Italia Network's tenth anniversary is the best opportunity to accomplish it. Before starting our conversation, however, I have a surprise for both my mother here and for all of you watching. I'm not saying anything, let me just show you some vintage footage and then we'll chat about it when we're done.

Composed and ritualistic bowing, smiles and then thrashing. The oriental world will never cease to amaze us. Centuries-old traditions still represent inviolable rules of life, but in the spectacle you are admiring there is none of this: it is an exhibition of Aikidō, a very modern genre of Japanese wrestling, whose official birth certificate dates only from 1945. In the early days, its technique was taken up only by a select few. Today, say the faithful, the time has come for it to spread among the people.
One against all, the system of collective defence.
Aikidō comprises 2,664 defensive and offensive techniques that can be practised standing or sitting. The result for the adversary is in any case deadly: physical strength, muscle training, agility, intelligence. All important and essential even against an armed opponent.
Here's a representative of the fairer sex, knocking down a colleague who is theoretically stronger than her. The secret is to train the body and mind to create perfect harmony. When we make a movement, the body acts first and then

the mind. Aikidō teaches instead to use the mind before the body. It is a question of achieving a perfect harmony between the spirit, the mind and the body. Aikidō, in short, invites us mainly to meditate.
A competition to the death, so to speak, between two women. No scratching and no grabbing by the hair. Aikidō does not allow it. Each movement requires coordination of intelligence with physical effort, an absolute balance of all the movements.
Finally the master confronts two disciples at the same time and regularly knocks them to the ground. Evidently they had not meditated enough in the first place.[1]

[SC] "What a nice surprise, eh folks? The year was 1968, the venue the *Dojo Centrale* in Rome: Tada sensei in action with his main students of the time. In the first part of the video we see Sensei throwing Gianni Cesaratto, Danilo Chierchini and Lino Lepore, among others. Then there is Mrs Carla Simoncini, who resolves some matrimonial issues by hacking up her husband Danilo Chierchini. After that there is a short clip showing Haru Onoda demonstrating some techniques with Makiko Nakakura, and lastly comes the segment featuring Tada sensei.

"This was the pioneers' Aikidō. How does it feel to see this video? Out of the blue, tell me all about it!"

[CS] "I didn't even know this film existed… but I remember the demonstration perfectly. It was one of the many we did to promote the budding Aikido movement. It gave me an enormous pleasure to see it again, especially because it was a completely different Carla: she was so many years younger! I liked her.

"I liked myself, that's the truth. I would put fire into every demonstration so that at least one spark would reach

---

[1] Istituto Luce video, available on YouTube at: https://youtu.be/D5h83A3eZKM

someone in the audience.

"Let me mention the most important demonstration I ever took part in. It made me really proud of myself and my colleagues of the time, who had been exposed to my 'fluttering' that made them whirl around, before being thunderously thrown onto the mat... I can't remember the year when it happened: too many years have gone by! It took place at the Palazzo dello Sport in Rome, at EUR, during the National Judo Championships. A group of the best students from the headquarters were trained to conduct an *enbukai* in between Jūdō competitions and it turned out to be a resounding success. We brought to the attention of those who practised a different martial art that strength and physical imbalance alone were not enough to prevail over an opponent. Those athletes did not even know what harmony and elegance, or large, circular movements were. We were showered with compliments and questions also came from the teachers who had accompanied their students to the competitions.

"I should point out that, as always, I was the only woman present. It was an unusual sight to see me tossing men around, often 20-30 kg heavier than me! These are really good memories. I realise that I have lived through a unique time and I don't know how many of the thousands of today's aikidoists can understand."

"Why did you choose Aikidō and what attracted you to this discipline?"[2]

"Nothing in particular, at least initially. I wanted to do some sport, but I was hardly attracted to anything, not even athletics, which at the time were regarded as suitable for women. I did swimming for fun, after taking some classes to

---

[2 3 4 5] This interview was carried out in an unusual way, thanks to the collaboration of our Aikido Italia Network friends, who sent us a series of questions. These are by Piernicola Vespri.

learn it.

"The enlightenment came to me when I saw Kawamukai sensei give a small demonstration in the State Monopolies hall. I must say that I was enchanted, because in the movements of the teacher I imagined Carla twirling with aerial movements, as in a dance. Kawamukai moved in a very ample and harmonious way, and I saw myself already on the mat, ready to practice an Aikidō combined with dancing, a passion of mine for years: merging the movements of one with the harmony of the other. I distinctly remember that it was what I felt like doing after seeing Master Kawamukai in action."

"How were Aikidō lessons conducted in those days? What was the normal format?"[3]

"We were very few, all or almost all of whom had no exercise to their credit. Little by little, we began to understand who had the means to go on and who would not continue. The sessions were exhausting, sometimes repetitive and not at all satisfying. We have all been beginners and we know how it works and what I'm talking about. We would have liked to be able to master the techniques we were taught as quickly as possible, to feel fulfilled by noticing a few glances from the teacher and being told we were good...

"After Kawamukai sensei, a sociable and friendly young man who had taught us the basics of how to be on the mat, Hiroshi Tada sensei took over, and the music changed. He took us by the hand and led us into a little piece of the East, both in our behaviour and way of practising. Tada sensei's aim was probably to create a small team and have students around him who could introduce to Italy a martial art that was unknown until then."

"What was your relationship with Tada sensei?"[4]

"Tada sensei had two faces: the one we saw on the mat was of frightening austerity. He didn't speak, he just said: 'Look!' If we asked him questions, owing to his poor knowledge of the Italian language, he would rather show us the technique again.

"What he conveyed as a person, though... If you were really into what we were doing, his energy stuck to you like a virus. You had a conscious feeling that you would be able to grow, even if you weren't capable of it yet. YES!!! Because you wanted to, there was this wonderful desire to participate and grow!!!

"And then we had Hiroshi Tada as a guest in our house, for dinner: a little chatting, a lot of eating and drinking... and once the wine made him let his guard down a little, he would come up with witty words or questions about our European world that he wasn't used to yet. He liked to eat, he liked to drink and, what little he could, to converse.

"He was, however, a reserved man, closed in his own world and religion, which he believed to be Aikidō. I don't say this to boast, but at that time I think I was the closest person to him, even though I was a woman. Perhaps it was a consequence of my innate sociability, but it also happened because I did not worship him as others did. I just followed him and copied him with my eyes and mind... He lived alone in a small room attached to the dōjō in Via Eleniana. Sometimes I would visit him in the mornings to chat and not make him feel too lonely."

"What were the main difficulties for you? Some of them you already mentioned, such as the lack of physical preparation."[5]

"I think they were those that anyone who started Aikidō felt: we were faced with completely new things, and furthermore we were dealing with practices and subjects that at least up to that point had had nothing to do with the West. As I said before, when you approach Aikidō, either you find that something, that sort of sixth sense necessary to go on, or Aikidō is better abandoned, since it becomes merely a physical exercise."

"I've never seen Carla in action, I've only watched her in a few very short period films, but the consensus is that she was quite skilled. How would you define your Aikidō? At the time, quoting from the articles in *Aikido*, the magazine of the Italian Aikikai, all you would read in relation to female aikidoists was 'Grace, harmony and effectiveness in this technique, to the point of not being out of place in front of her male colleagues'. Such were the descriptions of nine out of ten photos in the association's magazine in the 1970s. What do you think of your Aikidō from that time?"[6]

"As I have already mentioned, I have always been training among men. At the most, there were a few women who started practising and then disappeared without anyone ever knowing why. My Aikidō was the same as everyone's Aikidō. I have never considered myself or behaved as if I were

---
[6] Paolo Bottoni

part of the so-called weaker sex. I have Tada sensei to thank for this, as he never did anything to make me feel as such. He treated me like all the others, without compliments or special kindness. I took *ukemi* during the explanations like everyone else. I had learned to take long and high falls... in short, many of my male colleagues did not manage to achieve half of what I was learning, and I must say without much effort. It came naturally to me, maybe I have some Japanese ancestors [laughs].

"I gave beatings, I even broke a few bones and I kept going. I've never been scared of getting hurt, although it did happen once: I injured my knee while I was receiving a kotegaeshi, when my foot got caught between two tatami mats and the ligament almost snapped.

"What are my thoughts on the difference between the Aikidō of years gone by and the situation today? I could talk for hours about what I think. For a long time now, I did not follow the path of Aikidō and how the art progressed over the years. The pain of having to leave when I could have done so much for myself and for those I could have supported as a teacher was enormous. Let me be clear, I did not run away, I was kicked out. However, I am only telling you one thing: I no longer can see what we were taught by a REAL teacher.

"Everyone has their own way of practising, which reflects the various steps of learning, but one should not bastardise what we have been taught. Of course you can put in your own when you have reached a higher level of technical mastery, but you should not try to become a guru or present yourself as the bearer of the divine word... I compare it to ballet: have you ever seen a ballet dancer perform their choreography the way they want to? Nowadays I see a lot of people adorned with plumes and ambition. This has turned what it used to be into a bunch of clubs where everyone is trying to excel the others... Naturally I am referring to the situation in Italy. I don't have adequate knowledge of the situation abroad. And I am going to shut up here!!!"

"How did you experience these pioneering times in a very male-dominated environment and practice?"[7]

"It was male-oriented because there were many men, but they never treated me with condescension or put me in a position to think that my movements were more feminine than normal. There is no difference between those who practice Aikidō well, being a man or a woman, because strength does not exist in Aikidō."

"In connection with the above, what were the reactions of friends and colleagues outside the practice when they learned that you had started this martial discipline?"[8]

"Well, as a woman I've always been considered a bit out of the ordinary. This was something I never gave much thought to, because it is something that has accompanied me throughout my life. As I progressed in my training, however, with the improvements I made through the many demonstrations and seminars I took part in... friends and acquaintances who had the opportunity to see me were amazed: remember that this was in the sixties and I was the only woman among a group of men in what was considered a male activity. No one ever noticed the slightest difference in the way the men behaved towards me or I towards them."

"Have you ever managed to practice as an equal, i.e. without the feeling that men were holding back or were distracted by the fact that you were a woman?"[9]

"Absolutely, without any trouble. I can tell you a

[7,8] Carlo Caprino

little anecdote that proves the opposite. Gianni Cesaratto, a very dear friend of mine, used to keep away from me when we were practising in pairs. It was a laugh, because he was a tall, big and strong man, I was small and slender but with effective techniques. Well, to tell the truth, I think he was afraid."

"Let's gossip. Who was the prettiest hunk, the most beautiful lady and the most naughty rascal?"[10]

"The most handsome was Tada sensei! The most beautiful lady was myself, since I was the only woman. Who was the naughty one? Hardly anyone... I was Danilo Chierchini's wife and they didn't dare. Later I was told by Fabio Mongardini, another dear friend, that at that time they were all a bit in love with me. At any rate, on the mat there

---

[9] Gabriele Di Camillo

[10] Carlo Cocorullo

was absolute integrity everywhere, no one dared to attempt anything other than martial arts, also because Tada sensei was quite strict in that regard."

[SC] "Listen, I am going to ask you the next question, since I already know the answer. Can you tell us why you were not promoted to 2nd dan the first time you took the test?"

"Of course, it's a very funny thing, and I'm going to tell it straight now, even though for me at the time it was the source of great distress. We are in 1972, during the summer seminar of the Italian Aikikai in Desenzano del Garda. After having taken my nidan exam - an exhausting test which I believed I had done well, being the only woman with seven men - at the moment of handing over the diploma I was given a sheet of paper and offered an explanation which left me dumbfounded and without the energy to even bow and collect the paper: Tada sensei had given me a 'provisional' nidan, which meant that I would have to retake the exam a month later.

"I got up, didn't pick up my diploma, and ran to the women's changing room. A few minutes later I was followed by Tada sensei, who had left the mat after stopping the handing out of diplomas, something I don't think he has ever done again for anyone (by sneaking into the women's changing room, incidentally!). He came in and asked me why I hadn't collected my diploma.

"My answer was: 'I don't want it... because it's not fair, I don't think I've done anything less than what others have done. On the contrary, I've done better, as always'. And he replied: 'I expected more from you. You went dancing last night and you didn't behave the way I thought you would'. Well, I think he did it to get back at me... At the same time, afterwards, when my anger had subsided, I realised that he had big plans for me."

[SC] "Different times."

"Different times, for sure. Better ones, sorry Simone. Because we did Aikidō with feeling, without any ulterior motive, and we carried out what a great teacher taught us."

"What have you been able to express about yourself within your Aikidō? What has this discipline given you?"[11]

"Very much so. First, self-confidence, and not so much because I thought that if attacked in the street I would be able to defend myself. This confidence came from knowing that I could do it. I had entered a purely male art and had no difficulty in settling in. This important recognition came from both the teacher and fellow practitioners, I always felt at home. I recognise that Aikidō has strengthened my character, which was already strong, but not yet well defined. Over the years I have become a better and more positive person, I have experienced the joy of teaching adults and children. I found that I enjoyed teaching, but never as much as practising."

"Is there anything about Aikidō that you brought into your daily life once you stopped practising it physically and if so, what?"[12]

"My practice ended, but all that was harmonious, that had become part of my life, remained. What I started and carried on doing passed through my son. This is the strength I have left him."

"What do you think about Aikidō as a career?"[13]

---

[11] Antonella De Nuscis
[12] Marco Rubatto

"There is no such thing as being a professional in Aikidō, it is a characteristic of sports which serve other purposes, not at all those of a martial art. In my opinion, Aikidō is all about the spirit and not much about reason, and perhaps this is why we Westerners cannot realise what it really is. I often asked Tada sensei and Ikeda sensei, who also used to come to dinner with Tada sensei at our house, to explain what it meant for them and they said: 'For us Aikidō is a religion, not a sport'. And we Westerners have never been able to make these things our own, because we were not born and bred in a culture similar to theirs."

[SC] "Although, in the meantime, this applies in full to everyone, including them, because meanwhile the younger Japanese generations have come of age in much the same way as the Western ones. They too have experienced a fairly clean break with tradition."

---

[13] Bruno Brugnoli

The Lioness - Interview with Carla Simoncini

"Aikido is the Budō discipline with the most female participants, up to 30%. According to you, why is this the case? What is the reason for this strong presence?"[14]

"Pretty simple: because there is the harmony element, and the whole thing about moving wide and smooth. These are purely feminine elements, they are not particularly suitable for men."

"In the world of social media both male and female aikidoists are represented. However, there is a phenomenon whereby male aikidoists pretty much spend their time arguing about everything - from the colour of the belt, to associations, to where to put their pinkies in nikyo, and so on. Women never feature in these quarrels. How come it's only men who argue?"[15]

"Well, it's inherent to their nature. It's kind of funny to have to say it, because from the time they are children, men go around looking for a rifle to shoot others and the rifle keeps getting bigger... As they grow up, they leave the rifle behind and they look for leadership, they strive to get ahead. They always try to overpower others. This confrontational attitude should have no place in any sport, not to mention when a sport becomes an art...

"As such, men are not very suitable for Aikidō because of their way of being. I'm sorry, but I think that the few women who have gone on to achieve senior levels are the best. Unfortunately I haven't met many since I stopped. Many perhaps do not make it up because their teachers are not up to the task of taking them up. Many of the men who have achieved high honours - I don't know how authentic or handed over - would have done better to change discipline, perhaps switching to Jūdō or weightlifting... It is these who have distorted the true nature of Aikidō, transforming it into

---

[14-15] Nino Dellisanti

what they could practice.

"This is what I think. If I had continued, I don't know if I would have been able to endure what we later saw happen to genuine Aikidō. Because genuine Aikidō was what we practised: without any purpose, without running a club to get money out of. We didn't go around recruiting people to train, we weren't big-headed. We did Aikidō to do Aikidō. We more than earned the grades we were given through real sweat, the sweat of 4-5 hours of practice a day in order to become the bearers of what we wanted to transmit. My group certainly had an edge because it had a great teacher, Tada sensei."

"Were you developing personal aspirations for the future through Aikidō?"[16]

"I have already answered. I can only add that I tried to teach after they threw me out of the Aikikai, but I did not get on well with any association, because I would have liked to continue doing what I had acquired and it wasn't possible to do it in a way that respected the transmission of genuine Aikidō."

"I don't know if you are aware, but in that period *Yoseikan*-style Aikidō was already beginning to develop in Italy. What was the relationship between Yoseikan Aikidō and Aikikai students, if any? Or was there no relationship at all between the few who practised Aikidō in different styles at that time?"[17]

"When we started training, in Italy there was no knowledge of other associations where another style of Aikidō was practised. I am sorry, because I would have liked

---

[16] Andrea Re
[17] Adriano Amari

to engage with a different school and way of thinking, but this possibility was never offered to us."

"What were exams like at the time? Were they a long affair? Did Tada sensei ask for lots of techniques? Were they a marathon or a simple task?"[18]

"They were a marathon indeed. There was a booklet containing all the names of the techniques and the preparation was based on that. Not one technique was left out. The preparation was long, very hard and exhausting. When I think back to the test for my provisional 2nd dan, that lasted an hour and three quarters. It was insane.
"You never took it easy at the exams, they were like a hard, continuous workout in all forms, with direct and unceremonious attacks. As there were always large groups of examinees, there were only a few seconds to catch one's breath before moving on to the next technique, which was sharply called for by Tada sensei. He followed everyone at 360 degrees, inexorably, eyes like an ant... I should add that he was the one who decided who was going to be tested: many were left at the post for some time before becoming shodan."

[SC] "Times have changed, definitely, and this brings us to Claudio Regoli's question: 'Was it better before or is it better now?'."

"This is a question that if he is from the old days he should not even have asked..."

[SC] "He made it on purpose because he's from the old days all right!"

"Well, then we always come back to the same point:

---

[18] Piernicola Vespri

are we talking about genuine Aikidō, about what it was, or what it has become? The one that was, included hard, exhausting and lengthy examinations covering all the techniques. If someone decided to modify it, to make it less demanding, to soften it bit by bit, then I am sorry, my dear ones, you are no longer doing Aikidō."

[SC] "These are issues that are currently very much felt. We went through this pioneering phase, characterised by a form of training that was first of all physical, very intense, a phase of non-questioning, of enjoying the practice for what it was, non-philosophically… and then gradually, as in all things, the movement developed. As disciplines spread, so many more questions emerge. This phenomenon has happened worldwide. Today many people complain because Aikidō is experiencing, to tell it straight, a serious crisis in terms of vocation. This is, first of all, because by dint of softening the practice, of making it ever more open, ever more user-friendly, it has gradually become something that has everything and nothing inside.

"Now I have a question from an old colleague of yours, the only one we have online today. It comes from Claudio Pipitone, whom we greet: 'Carla, seeing that we both received the shodan from Tada sensei back in 1969 and that we are quite close in age, the first question that arises spontaneously to me is whether you still feel the influence in your daily life of those teachings you received and of the very exacting practice that we carried out at that time with Tada sensei'."

"Greetings, Claudio, first and foremost. Well, if the question means if I'd like to go back to the old days… yes, I would do it all again, because with my character I don't think I would ever have been influenced by the changes that took place in the following decades.

"And yes, I probably live on thanks to those

teachings, to those years dedicated with great effort to what I have harvested. I will never forget that I was the first female shodan in Italy and second dan in Europe: it made me grow up so much... Perhaps it is not very important for those who have not practised martial arts, but those who have lived through those periods and reached certain levels, I think they can understand.

"I don't think there has been another woman who has had this privilege. I had a wonderful school, a great teacher, excellent aikidoists to train with, who were always there for me, who always admired me. And the first was Tada sensei himself, who said I was his best student. What can I say, I consider myself lucky in life to have been called that, it gave me a wealth of strength and perseverance. Later on, I had to experience the trauma of having to leave all that behind. Hard luck... my son carried on."

"How does it feel to be the subject of so much attention to date?"[19]

"I set aside any desire to receive attention as an aikidoist, or for the fact that I was a pioneer of this martial art, as I said before, the moment I could no longer be part of the Italian Aikikai. I dropped it when I had to leave the mat. What a pity.

"I dedicated myself to something else and it went very well. I managed to transpose a special experience into another special experience. More than likely, without the first one I would not have succeeded later in my work. It was instrumental in my personal growth, the growth of a woman who began practising Aikidō as a girl, continued for a few years, and then took what she could from this important experience and carried it into another life situation. Having been developed as a fighter, regardless of gender, has served me well both in my work and in the politics I have been

---
[19] Alessio Autuori

involved in."

[SC] "That is, in real life, which in the end is what matters. Otherwise, Budō becomes merely another hobby.
"Very well, Ma, thank you. Many thanks from me, and from all of the friends of Aikido Italia Network."

Copyright Simone Chierchini ©2020
All rights are reserved

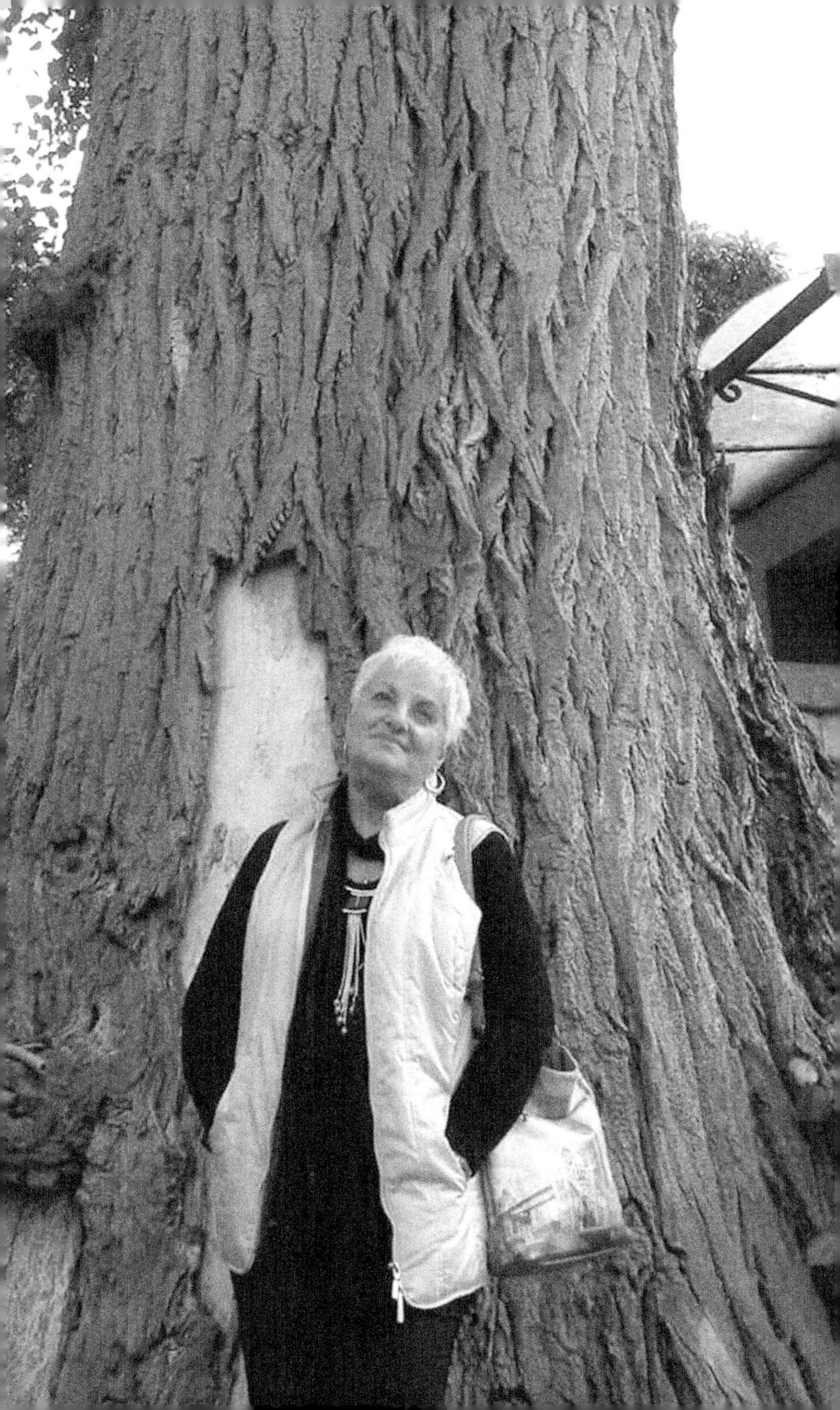

The Aiki Dialogues

1. The Phenomenologist - Interview with Ellis Amdur
2. The Translator - Interview with Christopher Li
3. The Wrestler - Interview with Rionne "Fujiwara" McAvoy
4. The Traveler - "Find Your Way" - Interview with William T. Gillespie
5. Inryoku - "The Attractive Force" - Interview with Gérard Blaize
6. The Philosopher - Interview with André Cognard
7. The Hermeticist - Interview with Paolo N. Corallini
8. The Heir - Interview with Hiroo Mochizuki
9. The Parent - Interview with Simone Chierchini

**Simone Chierchini: The Phenomenologist
Interview with Ellis Amdur**
The Aiki Dialogues - N. 1
Publisher: Aikido Italia Network Publishing
https://aikidoitalianetworkpublishing.com

Ellis Amdur is a renowned martial arts researcher, a teacher in two different surviving Koryū and a former Aikidō enthusiast. His books on Aikidō and Budō are considered unique in that he uses his own experiences, often hair-raising or outrageous, as illustrations of the principles about which he writes. His opinions are also backed by solid research and boots-on-the-ground experience. "The Phenomenologist" is no exception to that.

Simone Chierchini: The Translator - Interview with Christopher Li
The Aiki Dialogues - N. 2
Publisher: Aikido Italia Network Publishing
https://aikidoitalianetworkpublishing.com

Christopher Li is an instructor at the Aikido Sangenkai, a non-profit Aikidō group in Honolulu, Hawaii, on the island of Oahu. He has been training in traditional and modern Japanese martial arts since 1981, with more than twelve years of training while living in Japan. Chris calls himself a "hobbyist with a specialty", however, thanks to his research and writing he has made an important contribution to the understanding of modern Aikidō. His views on Aikidō, its history and future development are unconventional and often "politically incorrect" but he's not afraid to share them. This is not a book for those unwilling to discuss the official narrative of our art and its people.

Simone Chierchini: The Wrestler - Interview with Rionne McAvoy
The Aiki Dialogues - N. 3
Publisher: Aikido Italia Network Publishing
https://aikidoitalianetworkpublishing.com

From Taekwondo wonder kid to Karate State Champion, from Hiroshi Tada Sensei's Gessoji Dojo to the Aikikai Hombu Dojo and Yoshiaki Yokota sensei, Rionne "Fujiwara" McAvoy, a star in the toughest professional wrestling league in the world, Japan, has never been one for finding the easy way out.
In "The Wrestler", Rionne McAvoy tells his story in martial arts and explains his strong views on Aikido, physical training and cross-training and reveals where he wants to go with his Aikido.

**Simone Chierchini: The Traveler - Find Your Way
Interview with William T. Gillespie**
The Aiki Dialogues - N. 4
Publisher: Aikido Italia Network Publishing
https://aikidoitalianetworkpublishing.com

William T. Gillespie, the author of the book "Aikido in Japan and The Way Less Traveled", is a pioneer of Aikido in China. As the sign in his first Aikido Dojo in Los Angeles read, "Not even a million dollars can buy back one minute of your life". This is why W.T. Gillespie resigned from a professional career as a trial attorney in Los Angeles, also leaving his position as an assistant instructor in Furuya sensei's dojo. He cast aside all the enviable benefits and considerable comforts of life in Southern California to move to Tokyo to devote himself to intensively study Aikido at the Aikikai World Headquarters. Currently a 6th Dan Aikikai, his martial arts adventures in Japan and beyond to South East Asia, Korea and even The People's Republic of China became a fantastic journey of self-discovery and personal development that continues to unfold.

**Simone Chierchini: Inryoku - The attractive Force
Interview with Gérard Blaize**
The Aiki Dialogues - N. 5
Publisher: Aikido Italia Network Publishing
https://aikidoitalianetworkpublishing.com

Gérard Blaize, the first non-Japanese Aikido expert to receive the rank of 7th dan Aikikai, spent five and a half years in Japan where he studied Aikido at the Hombu Dōjō in Tōkyō. In 1975, he met Michio Hikitsuchi, one of the most respected personal students of the founder of Aikido Morihei Ueshiba, and followed his sole guidance until his teacher's death in 2004. Hikitsuchi Sensei was a Shinto priest as well as a high ranked martial artist; in 1957, he received from O-sensei the Masakatsu Bo Jutsu diploma. Furthermore, in 1969 he was personally awarded the 10th Dan rank by O-sensei.
Gérard Blaize has inherited and is still carrying the legacy of Hikitsuchi's holistic Aikido to this day.

**Simone Chierchini: The Philosopher
Interview with André Cognard**
The Aiki Dialogues - N. 6
Publisher: Aikido Italia Network Publishing
https://aikidoitalianetworkpublishing.com

André Cognard is one of the most authoritative voices in contemporary international Budo. Born in 1954 in France, he approached the world of martial arts at a very young age, dedicating himself to the intensive practice of various traditional Japanese disciplines. In 1973 he met Hirokazu Kobayashi sensei, a direct disciple of O-sensei Morihei Ueshiba, a decisive event that led to his decision to devote himself exclusively to the practice and teaching of Aikido. He received the rank of 8th Dan and on the death of his mentor inherited the leadership of the international academy Kokusai Aikido Kenshukai Kobayashi Hirokazu Ryu – KAKKHR. An "itinerant" teacher, a profound connoisseur of Japan and its traditions, André Cognard brings worldwide a technique – the Aikido of his Master; a human message – Aikido at the service of all; a spiritual message – Aikido which, like Man, reconnects with itself when it simply becomes Art.

**Simone Chierchini: The Hermeticist
Interview with Paolo N. Corallini**
The Aiki Dialogues - N. 7
Publisher: Aikido Italia Network Publishing
https://aikidoitalianetworkpublishing.com

Paolo N. Corallini has been practising the Art of Aikido since 1969 and during his career he has held numerous positions in this art at national and international level. He is currently a 7th dan Aikido Shihan and the Technical Director of Takemusu Aikido Association Italy.
Author of many conferences on Aikido and its Spirituality, he has written 6 volumes on this martial art. A scholar of Eastern philosophies and religions such as Taoism, Shintoism, Esoteric Buddhism and Sufism, he loves the world of chivalric tradition in general and the Knights Templar in particular.
In "The Hermeticist" Corallini sensei brings the reader from Iwama and his meeting with Morihiro Saito sensei to the complex interweaving between the different pedagogies in Aikido; from his memories of the man Morihiro Saito to the future of Aikido and much much more, always presenting his learned and refined approach to the sense of what exists below the visible level of Aikido.

Adriano Amari: The Heir
Interview with Hiroo Mochizuki
The Aiki Dialogues - N. 8
Publisher: Aikido Italia Network Publishing
https://aikidoitalianetworkpublishing.com

Hiroo Mochizuki is the heir of a samurai family.
Creator of Yoseikan Budo, he is a world-renowned expert in Japanese martial arts.
Son of the famous teacher Minoru Mochizuki, who is considered a Japanese national treasure and was also a direct student of Jigoro Kano and Morihei Ueshiba, the successor of a line of samurai, Hiroo Mochizuki was inspired by his forefathers combative spirit to create Yoseikan Budo.
He adapted the philosophy, pedagogy and traditional practice of martial arts to a new modern environment, as well as to contemporary combat techniques.
Besides practicing Mixed Martial Arts before people knew what MMA was, Hiroo Mochizuki has one of the most impressive records in the martial world.

Simone Chierchini

THE TEACHER

**Interview with
LIA SUZUKI**

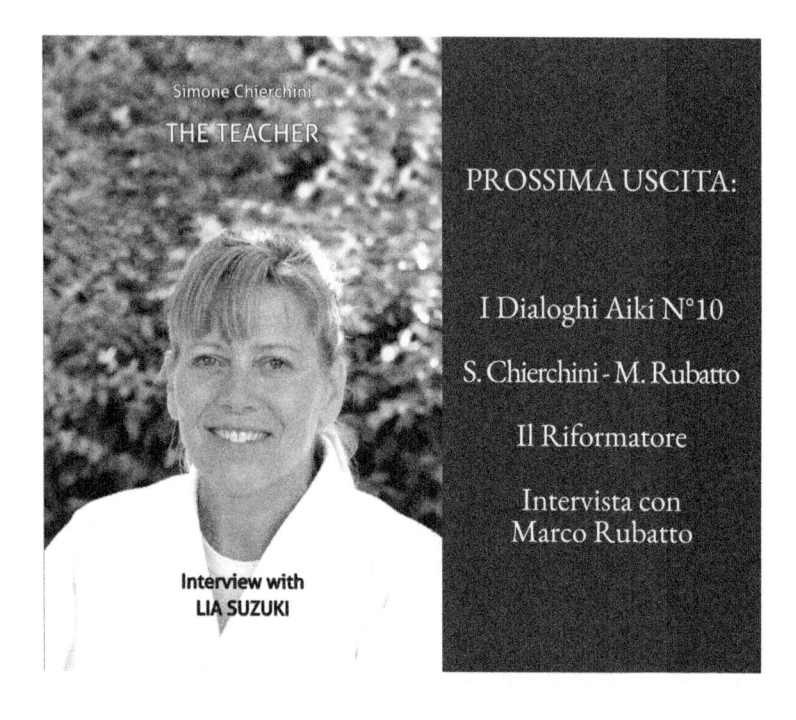

PROSSIMA USCITA:

I Dialoghi Aiki N°10

S. Chierchini - M. Rubatto

Il Riformatore

Intervista con
Marco Rubatto

Lia Suzuki, founder and director of Aikido Kenkyukai International USA, began her Aikido training in 1982 under William Gleason. She soon moved to Japan to train with Yoshinobu Takeda, one of Seigo Yamaguchi's most accomplished students.

She lived in Japan and trained extensively in Aikido from 1987 to 1996. At the urging of Takeda shihan, Lia sensei returned to establish dojos in the USA in 1996. She currently holds the rank of 6th dan Aikikai and travels extensively as a guest instructor, conducting Aikido seminars in dojos around the world.

Over the years, Lia sensei has dedicated her training to promoting inclusion in the world of Aikido and increasing the popularity of Aikido among young people, Gen Z and Millennials.

Since founding AKI USA in 1996, she has also led various philanthropic and social projects and initiatives.

More recently, through her work at the Virtual Dojo, she has provided Aikido teachers and students with the resources they needed to navigate the challenging times we are facing, helping them navigate and adapt to the new world of online training.

Printed in Great Britain
by Amazon